WALKING ON
THE ISLE OF WIGHT

About the Author

Paul Curtis is an enthusiastic newcomer to guidebook writing, having enjoyed writing a popular blog about a 2008 solo cycling trip from Boston to San Diego. He has a great passion for travelling, particularly long-distance hiking and cycling, and has complemented an office-based career with getting away to as many wonderful places as possible in his free time. He fell in love with the Isle of Wight on his first visit in 2008, and returned periodically to walk there before making it his home in 2011.

In addition to his US adventure, Paul has cycled from Amsterdam to Sarandë in Albania and from Calais to Istanbul, hiked across Switzerland and has completed several long-distance walking trails in the UK including the North Downs Way, the Thames Path and the Hertfordshire Way. He is a solo, romantic explorer in the Wainwright tradition and believes that guidebooks should first and foremost be about finding the most beautiful routes and providing precise, accurate descriptions.

Paul is a qualified proofreader and trainee copy-editor. He lives on the Isle of Wight and this is his first book.

WALKING ON
THE ISLE OF WIGHT

by Paul Curtis

2 POLICE SQUARE, MILNTHORPE, CUMBRIA LA7 7PY
www.cicerone.co.uk

© Paul Curtis 2013
First edition 2013
ISBN: 978 1 85284 661 9

Printed by KHL Printing, Singapore.
A catalogue record for this book is available from the British Library.
All photographs are by the author unless otherwise stated.

For my friend Ruth

Acknowledgements

Thanks to the Hampshire and Isle of Wight Wildlife Trust for their advice on the Wildlife section of this guide.

Advice to Readers

While every effort is made by our authors to ensure the accuracy of guidebooks as they go to print, changes can occur during the lifetime of an edition. If we know of any, there will be an Updates tab on this book's page on the Cicerone website (www.cicerone.co.uk), so please check before planning your trip. We also advise that you check information about such things as transport, accommodation and shops locally. Even rights of way can be altered over time. We are always grateful for information about any discrepancies between a guidebook and the facts on the ground, sent by email to info@cicerone.co.uk or by post to Cicerone, 2 Police Square, Milnthorpe LA7 7PY, United Kingdom.

Front cover: Scratchell's Bay and the Needles (Walk 9)

CONTENTS

Route symbols on OS map extracts

~   route   (↟)   start point

~   link route   (↟)   finish point

(↟)   start/finish point   ◀   route direction

(↟)   alternative start/finish point

Features on the overview map

🏭   urban area   ▦▦▦   downland area

For OS legend see OS maps.

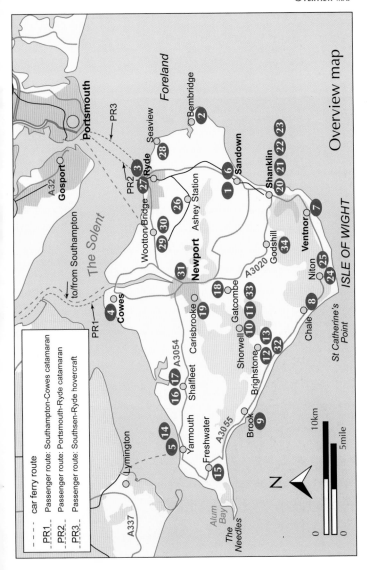

Overview map

Beach, Hamstead Point (Walk 4)

INTRODUCTION

Steephill Cove (Walk 7)

It is suprising that, in spite of the Isle of Wight's beauty and elegance, this peaceful and perfect-sized island is often dismissed simply as a place to go for a long weekend or somewhere to send children on school trips. Perhaps it is because many visitors tend not to penetrate the island beyond the resorts and the tourist attractions. But those with curiosity are likely to fall in love with this place; its variety of scenery and understated aesthetic qualities are appreciated mainly by those on foot, with almost everywhere being accessible courtesy of the green buses which stand out on the landscape. The Isle of Wight is made for walking!

Nearly half the island is a designated Area of Outstanding Natural Beauty, but this is misleading as almost the entire island can rightly be called beautiful. While there are jaw-dropping views such as those from the magnificent coastline of West Wight, St Boniface, Culver and Brading Downs, around St Catherine's Point and the Needles, there is also a gentler, more intimate beauty at countless locations unknown even by many islanders, such as remote Newtown Harbour, an 'undiscovered' balcony trail near Gatcombe, and even the scenic path linking urban Carisbrooke and Newport.

Bembridge Down cliffs (Walk 1)

The island's default scenery is graceful, undulating downland, very attractive to the eye, which means that if you walk in any direction for up to 5 miles you would almost certainly glimpse the sea! Tree-lovers are also well catered for, with the large and lonely Brighstone Forest being particularly attractive, situated on top of the magnificent West Wight ridge of downs and offering enchanting sea views from its southern fringe. And sea-lovers will be enamoured with the Coastal Path: simply a stunner! Only thrill-seeking walkers or those not interested in anything except Alpine scenery would be disappointed with the Isle of Wight.

There are an incredible 525km (326 miles) of footpaths on an island of just 381 square kilometres (147 square miles), and there are more footpaths and bridleways than roads. Such a choice of where to walk means that walkers can experience all the diversity the island has to offer – not only scenery but also many of the 2000 or so listed buildings – and that the trails are not too crowded, except on very popular routes in high season.

The Isle of Wight (IoW) is an ideal size for a short break – not so small that visitors can become familiar with it in under a week, yet small enough to walk from Bembridge on the east coast to the Needles on the west coast in a single day. Away from the few towns and sometimes cheesy coastal resorts (themselves not lacking in charm), the IoW is genuinely a walker's paradise: an overused term, but definitely applicable in this case. This is not just because of the consistently attractive, varied scenery and preponderance of footpaths, but also because of a particularly mild, temperate climate, exceptionally good access to walks via public transport, and optimum levels of safety – the last of which makes it an especially good destination for beginners and families to try some walking.

The fact that the Isle of Wight is not teeming with walkers all year round is everyone else's loss and your gain. Happy walking!

GEOGRAPHY AND LANDSCAPE

The island is diamond-shaped, about 37km (23 miles) from Bembridge (east) to the Needles (west), and 21km (13 miles) from Cowes (north) to St Catherine's Point (south). This makes it small enough to cross by car in about an hour, but large enough to offer a huge variety of interest in terms of both natural landscape and towns and villages. First-time visitors may be surprised at just how close the mainland seems: from Yarmouth it is only 1.5km (1 mile) away. On clear days and from lofty vantage points, the mainland coastline can be seen as far as Bournemouth and the Isle of Purbeck to the west and Beachy Head to the east – which perhaps contributes to disagreements over whether the island is more a part of southwest or southeast England. But on the south-facing coasts the open sea seems endless; the eye looks towards France but never sees it.

View from Bembridge Point (Walks 2, 28, 31)

11

There are seven major towns on the island: Cowes and East Cowes on the north-central coast, Ryde on the northeast coast, the resorts of Sandown, Shanklin and Ventnor on the southeast coast, and Newport in the centre. Yarmouth is a small town on the northwest coast, and ill-defined Freshwater comprises much of the far west. Unlike many towns on the mainland, each feels unique and has a special character. Villages and hamlets are numerous and all maintain a distinct identity, derived from a sense of location and history: they are much more than their constituent streets and buildings. Some, notably Godshill and Shorwell, are decidedly photogenic, with an abundance of thatched cottages and attractive stone houses.

But it is the downland that really makes the island great, and it is thoroughly explored in these walks. There can be said to be three major stretches: from Newport east to the sea (St George's Down to Culver Down); the 'southeast downs' which form an arc around the village of Wroxall; and from Carisbrooke southwest to the so-called 'Back of the Wight' (the southwest coastline from Chale to Freshwater Bay and the villages just behind). The key to mastering the geography of the island is familiarity with the downs!

The sea around the entire island, both the Solent and English Channel proper, is notoriously rough and claimed a number of ships and lives particularly in the 18th and 19th centuries. The south is very prone to cliff

Alum Bay (Walk 9)

Gore Cliffs, Blackgang (Walk 7)

erosion and landslips because of its secondary layer of gault clay (known as 'blue slipper'). When rain permeates the gault it moves forward, causing the instability. These processes, together with rising sea levels after the last ice age, created the Undercliff between Ventnor and Niton; and today erosion and landslips still cause problems, not least Coastal Path diversions – the island is continually getting smaller! The Blackgang Chine attraction, located on a cliff-top near Niton, has particularly suffered over the years, and in 1928 a major landslip a little to the east caused an irreparable breach in the old Niton to Blackgang road.

But erosion is not all bad. One positive by-product is that it constantly reveals new fossils. The island is nicknamed the 'Dinosaur Isle' because of the large number of fossils that may be found, especially on the beaches at Compton Bay (see Walk 9) and Yaverland (see Walk 1). Along the Back of the Wight erosion has enlarged several 'chines' (a local term for a breach in a sea-cliff) and created caves, such as those below Tennyson Down.

The north of the island has a firmer geological foundation, its hard clays supporting a surprisingly large and varied range of woodland (some ancient), such as eerie Parkhurst Forest, America Wood and numerous smaller woods, although deforestation has occurred regularly throughout the ages. Much planting of non-native but red-squirrel-friendly trees has taken place over the past 100 years (both conifer, such as Scots pine, and broadleaf, such as sycamore), but the trend now is to increase the proportion of native species while also increasing biodiversity.

13

Unusually, all rivers flow north. The Medina and Western Yar are remarkable for their oversized estuaries (from Newport to Cowes, and Freshwater to Yarmouth respectively). The Eastern Yar flows from Niton to Bembridge, and Newtown River and Wootton Creek are fed by multiple streams, such as the Caul Bourne in the case of the former.

The National Trust has a very strong presence on the island, owning and maintaining precious areas such as Newtown Harbour and the Needles Batteries, and there are a total of 41 Special Sites of Scientific Interest (SSSIs), which include woods, downs and marshes. All in all, the landscape features of the Isle of Wight are expertly protected, whether by the National Trust, Forestry Commission or the council.

A POTTED HISTORY

There are two principal theories as to the origin of 'Wight'. The root word may have originated in the Iron Age and been subsequently altered many times, including by the Romans who called the island Vectis; the original definition apparently was 'little appendage'. Another theory is that 'Vectis' is unrelated to past or previous names, and that the root of the modern name derived from the original name for Carisbrooke: Wihtgarsburh – possibly named after a Saxon king.

For the vast majority of the Earth's history, there was no Isle of Wight as such, as the island we know today was part of the mainland. Dinosaurs arrived some 125 million years ago when the region was then situated near the Equator, and today 'Dinosaur Isle' is world-renowned for its fossils, especially along Compton Bay, the beach at Yaverland and Bouldnor Cliffs. Finds are often not particularly significant, commonly fossilised iguanodon footprints, but skeletons of Hypsilophodon and Neovenator salerii have been discovered.

It was only during the past 8000–10,000 years that an island was formed, caused by the sea flooding the Solent valley at the end of the last ice age and subsequently eroding the coastlines. In those days, the island was wholly covered by oak and elm, and it was only in about 3000BC that the sedentary agricultural lifestyle started to replace the hunter-gatherer way of life – trees were felled and cereals cultivated, allowing more complex societies to develop on the fledgling island.

Trading routes were soon established over the downs, and today's walkers will be reminded of life in this Neolithic period by communal burial mounds, known as barrows, alongside these routes, notably on the Back of the Wight. The Long Stone near Mottistone is a more tangible ancient monument; it is likely that Neolithic people met here to discuss and debate.

The islanders knew they were no match for the Roman army when they invaded in AD43, led by Vespasian – the future emperor. The island never really flourished under Roman rule; seven or eight villas were built for the wealthy – the ones at Brading and Newport have been preserved and are open to the public – but no towns or roads were constructed as they were on the mainland. However, one industry started during Roman times was to last for centuries: stone quarrying at Binstead. Winchester and Chichester cathedrals, as well as the island's first Quarr Abbey, were built using Binstead stone.

After the Romans left in the fifth century, Saxon King Cerdic conquered the island. A large Jutish migration around the same time probably led to intermarriage between the Germanic tribes; certainly Cerdic's nephew Stuf was known as a Jute who became the first recognised king of the island.

This Jutish kingdom ended with the bloody invasion by Caedwalla, King of Wessex, in 685, who slaughtered much of the population and forced surviving islanders to convert to Christianity, apparently in line with the whole of the rest of Britain.

Viking raids posed a problem towards the end of the Dark Ages, the island briefly serving as an important strategic base; but with the invasion of the generally more civilised and wealthy Normans in 1066, and the construction of Carisbrooke Castle shortly after, the security of the island against further attack was greatly enhanced (and to this day there has not been any subsequent, fully successful invasion). Formal governance created official ties with the mainland: William FitzOsbern – close relative of

Old Rectory Mansion, Brading (Walks 27, 31, 33)

Hoy Monument (Walks 11, 25)

the Conqueror – became the first Lord of the Isle of Wight, which became a hereditary title after Henry I granted it to FitzOsbern's nephew Richard de Redvers (the designer of Newport). The last lord was Isabella de Fortibus, who was either persuaded or coerced into selling the island to Edward I, and thus it was fully incorporated into the kingdom. Governors were appointed thereafter until the role was abolished in 1995.

Constant concern about a foreign invasion was proved justified when in 1377 the French launched devastating raids on the ports of Newtown, Yarmouth and Newport – but failure to capture Carisbrooke Castle necessitated their withdrawal. This was 25 years after the Black

Death had already decimated much of the population. After subsequent attacks, Yarmouth Castle was built by Henry VIII, but the island continued to generally decline until the 1600s, when a fledgling shipbuilding industry in Cowes proved successful and Newport began a gradual renaissance. The 1700s saw the rebuilding in grand style of the old manor houses at Gatcombe, Appuldurcombe and Swainston by their wealthy owners, perhaps reflecting relatively prosperous times for both the island and the country as a whole.

By the turn of the 1800s there was a new fashion for leisure travel among the well-to-do. In 1796 regular Solent crossings started between Portsmouth and Ryde, and several distinguished visitors came to discover what the island had to offer. Tennyson relocated here for several years; and Dickens, Keats, Darwin and several other notables all visited. Two of today's premier attractions opened in this early period: the gorge of Shanklin Chine in 1817 and Blackgang Chine amusement park in 1843; and the multicoloured sands of Alum Bay quickly became popular by word of mouth. Royalty were soon to get in on the act: King George IV was a member of the original Royal Yacht Club which founded Cowes Week in 1826, and his niece Queen Victoria fell in love with 'dear, modest, unpretentious' Osborne House up the road in Whippingham. All this time smuggling was rife on the island, and it is said that the majority of the islanders were involved in some way with the rackets. Also, just as the tourists were beginning to arrive, native species such as red and fallow deer were becoming extinct.

Railways arrived in the 1860s, and by 1900 there was an extremely comprehensive system in place, reaching Cowes, Freshwater and Ventnor – which had two stations! This led to once tiny fishing hamlets reinventing themselves as important resorts, and consequently a much greater influx of visitors. New seaside pleasure piers started to provide entertainment to the public, and soon the island acquired a reputation for being a destination that all could enjoy. The island went from strength to strength in the early half of the 20th century, its infrastructure dramatically improving. During the Second World War the island was relatively unscathed, in part due to the old Palmerston Forts – such as the Needles Batteries – being restocked with contemporary weapons, so providing an effective defence; but Cowes suffered a major hit in 1942, and the war saw over 200 casualties in total.

Due to under-use, the railway system was a victim of government cuts under Dr Beeching and was all but dismantled by 1966, but tourism continued to thrive until the 1980s. The world's first hovercraft service started across the Solent in 1965, and in 1970 hundreds of thousands of music-lovers descended on East Afton Down for the third Isle of Wight Festival to hear the likes of Jimi Hendrix and The Doors, severely straining infrastructure and causing locals and the council some alarm! By the 1990s, however, a wealthier British population had discovered cheap foreign holidays, and the island developed a somewhat lower profile. Perhaps consequently, these days a large number of visitors are older people seeking peace and quiet, and traditional food and attractions. In recent times the island has not been exempt from economic problems, not helped by the decline in family tourism, but islanders remain happy and resolute. Living here, you could not fail to be so!

SOCIETY

The 144,000 people of the Isle of Wight are a mixed bunch. In small villages such as Calbourne, Shorwell and Brighstone, the residents are typically older, comfortably off, and the epitome of Middle England. Whether 'overners' (the island word for outsiders) or 'caulkheads' (people born on the island, such as Sheila Hancock, Jeremy Irons and Phill Jupitus), they are as proud of their village as they are of their island. In the towns, where the majority of younger people live, the situation is a little more complex: at the time of writing, youth unemployment and a struggling economy have caused particular problems in Newport, Ryde and Sandown, and many of the brightest young people seek new opportunities on the mainland. A third type of resident is one who has a summer home here: Seaview, for example, is a village with a high proportion of second-homers. As a county, the average age of the island's population is significantly higher than the national average, and this margin is increasing all the time, which is a real economic concern for the coming years (in 2026 36% of the population is forecast to be over the current retirement age).

But despite these differences in the population, a small island almost by definition must have a sense of community, and there is a very strong one on the Isle of Wight. Serious crime is very rare; in fact, there is a distinct lack of 'edge' to the island, which perhaps reinforces the widely held notion that it is 'stuck in the 1950s'. The rather staid atmosphere today is presumably a great contrast with life

Brighstone (Walks 12, 13, 32)

before 'Victorianisation', when life in the fields was tough, smuggling was commonplace, and the forbidding coastline claimed numerous lives.

Arguably the main truly local event on the island's calendar is the annual Walking Festival fortnight in May, which culminates in 'Walk the Wight' day when thousands of people walk from Bembridge in the east to the Needles Park in the west for charity (shorter walks are also available). Walkers are given special permission to walk across some private land for the occasion. Much bigger events – such as the Isle of Wight Festival, its younger sibling Bestival, June's Round the Island yacht race, and August's Cowes Week – attract tens of thousands of visitors and keep the island in the spotlight.

Agriculture was the mainstay of the island's economy for centuries, but since Victorian times tourism has rivalled it. Although the era of the family fortnight holiday on the island is long dead, 'short-break' independent tourism is still at a respectable level and forecast to increase.

PRINCIPAL LOCATIONS

Alum Bay (Walks 5, 9, 15) has been a major attraction for as long as tourists have been visiting the island on account of its magnificent and uniquely multicoloured cliffs, the colouring arising from the presence of various sulphates created by the oxidation of pyrite (ferrous sulphide). It

is often said that there are 21 colours – although presumably what constitutes a colour is open to definition – and sand from the cliffs has been a traditional purchase ever since the early 19th century. A seasonal chairlift that has been in operation since 1971 transports visitors from the Needles Park down some 60m to the bay.

Bembridge (Walks 1, 2, 28, 31) is the most easterly settlement on the island and was, until the 1870s, a remote peninsula, due to the sea extending as far southwest as Brading. The medieval community relied primarily on stone exporting to survive, and the famous vessel the *Mary Rose* sank while trying to defend it from a French invasion in 1545 (the French left after realising they didn't have enough resources to conquer the island). The isolated community built a church in the 1820s (rebuilt 1840s), but proper development got underway from 1878 when a road and rail embankment was built to link it to nearby St Helens. A ferry service and pier complemented the village until the 1920s, when its heyday as a bustling tourist destination ended; the ferry was withdrawn, the pier demolished and the railway closed in 1953. Today's Bembridge is a rather sprawling village, but not unattractive. Look out for the rare 1929 K1 telephone kiosk in the high street.

There has been a settlement at **Brading** (Walks 27, 31, 33) since time immemorial, and until the 16th century it was a working port. After

View from Brading Down towards Shanklin (Walk 27)

much of the harbour was successfully drained in 1878, the town somewhat lost its prosperity. Today, though, 'Ye Kynge's Towne of Bradynge' should be on every visitor's list, and three of the walks in this guide pass through it. Of interest, from north to south, are the 12th-century church, adjacent 18th-century Old Town Hall, the 13th-century Rectory Mansion (allegedly the oldest building on the island), the Lilliput Doll and Toy Museum, the bull ring (bull baiting was outlawed only in 1835) and Brading Roman Villa, one of the most important Roman sites in the UK (30mins walk).

The pretty cottages on the slender, twisting high street are largely Victorian. Brading Day is celebrated on the first weekend of July to commemorate the granting of the town's first charter in 1285.

Brighstone (Walks 12, 13, 32) was called Brixton until the turn of the 20th century. It is a pretty enough place, and its Back of the Wight location is superb, sandwiched between dramatic downland and the sea. Three of the walks turn up North Street, which hosts the interesting little National Trust museum and equally quaint post office. The village pub is proudly named after three local churchmen who ended their careers as bishops.

Brook (Walks 8, 9) is very much a blink-and-you've-missed-it hamlet with no identifiable core. Charles Seely purchased most of the village in 1859, including Brook House, a family residence until 1970, built on the site of an earlier manor house visited by King Henry VII. Italian Unionist Garibaldi visited in 1864, and in 1901 Charles built Brook Hill House for his son Frank on a nearby hill; the house was subsequently owned by JB Priestley. The church was largely rebuilt in the 1860s, having been severely fire damaged.

Evidence suggests that **Carisbrooke** (Walks 18, 19) was the principal settlement in Anglo-Saxon times. So it is no surprise that after the Conquest it was here that the Normans constructed their castle. An upstart new rival called Newport emerged late in the 12th century, its river-valley location helping it to flourish, and today Carisbrooke is considered a Newport suburb, despite the distinct village-like feel along its high street.

Cowes (or West Cowes) (Walks 3, 4) is synonymous with all things nautical. It was here in August 1826 that the highly prestigious Royal Yacht Club, formed 11 years earlier and with King William IV as a founder member, held its first yachting regatta, starting an annual tradition which continues to this day. Cowes is positively buzzing during Cowes Week, and the sheer number of events, boats and participants make it a very special time to visit. The Royal Yacht Squadron, as the Club is now called, still calls Cowes its home (specifically Cowes Castle, originally a Tudor defence structure), and it is also the start and finish of the Round the Island race usually held every June. The town has medieval origins, but really came into its own in the 17th century, benefiting from passing trade and, later, shipbuilding (it is said that Cowes shipbuilders are

the original 'caulkheads'). Stately residences were built such as Northwood House, and Cowes Week and the coming of the railway in 1862 (the first on the island) cemented the fortunes of the town. Today, even outside Cowes Week, the high street and esplanade feel hip and lively.

East Cowes (Walks 3, 4) is separated from Cowes by the River Medina, but is quite literally linked to it by a chain ferry, and the town mimicked Cowes' fortunes from the 17th century. Notable buildings include Norris Castle and the all-but-demolished East Cowes Castle, the home of architect John Nash, who also designed the town's church and is buried in its churchyard. East Cowes continued to specialise in shipbuilding when its more glitzy neighbour turned to sailing. 'High society' and kudos came to East Cowes in a big way, however, when Victoria and Albert purchased and greatly extended Osborne House in the 1840s. The town centre is low key, but if you have an hour to spare it is pleasant to walk along the esplanade to the grounds of Norris Castle.

More a district than a town, **Freshwater** (Walks 5, 9, 14, 15, 19) is the largest urban settlement west of Cowes and Newport. It is made up of several hamlets, such as the old village itself, School Green, Norton Green, Middleton and Locksley; although the coastal resorts of Norton, Colwell, Totland and Freshwater Bay – and, in fact, the whole peninsula to the west of the Western Yar (technically

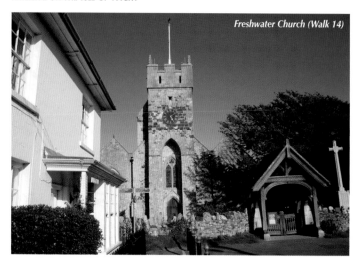
Freshwater Church (Walk 14)

an island in itself) – can also be included in a loose definition. Only disparate communities existed before the 19th century – the parish neatly consisted of Norton, Weston, Easton, Sutton (today's Freshwater Bay) and Middleton – and, as with the east-coast resorts, development was accelerated with the coming of the railway in 1889. Rather than an urban sprawl, however, there exist several charming pockets of countryside between the residential areas: Walk 15 gives a good introduction. Distinguished 17th-century scientist Robert Hooke was born here, but it is as the home of Alfred Lord Tennyson for several years that Freshwater is famed: his Farringford House still stands, and there is a striking monument to him on top of Tennyson Down.

Pronounced 'godzill' by locals, the village of **Godshill** (Walks 23, 32, 34) is one of the principal inland excursion destinations and so can become very crowded in summer. Nevertheless, a pretty place is a pretty place, and the tourists who visit are not likely to spoil one's enjoyment. The village consists of an attractive main street with numerous thatched buildings and a disproportionate number of tearooms. A visit to the model village (open since 1952) is well worthwhile, as is the ascent to the 14th-century church and the lovely thatched cottages close by. The church is remarkable for its 15th-century 'Lily Cross' painting, and is the second church on the site. The first was built shortly before the Norman Conquest, and the name Godshill came about because its foundations miraculously made their way from a different spot to their current hilltop location!

The island's capital, **Newport** (Walks 17, 18, 30, 31), is a small, relaxed place, but large enough to accommodate a high street featuring both chain and independent shops, and is worth a half-day's visit. The Minster on St Thomas' Square is Victorian, having replaced a 12th-century church, and the small but interesting and under-marketed Museum of Island History in the Guildhall should be visited (limited opening hours). Notable streets are Quay Street and Watchbell Lane, both explored on Walk 30. The town was founded around 1180 by Richard de Redvers, then Lord of the Island, as a port settlement near Carisbrooke, and it was he who introduced the grid system of streets that still exists today. Its heyday was in Georgian times, following the decline in fortune of nearby Newtown and prior to the growth of Ryde and Cowes.

Known as the Gateway to the Island, **Ryde** (Walks 2, 3, 27) is something of an enigma. The town does not exude sophistication and has clearly seen better days, but its idiosyncrasies are beguiling, and actually it possesses a wealth of fine early 19th-century architecture which goes largely unnoticed. Union Street, the steep commercial avenue ascending from the esplanade, was built in 1780 to link the villages of Lower and Upper Ryde. This helped form one town, which really came into its own in Victorian times, being the first stop for the thousands of people who came to the island for their holidays (the Portsmouth ferry started in 1825). The pier dates from 1814, the ornate iron balustrades being installed around 1880.

Prince Consort Building, Ryde (Walk 3)

23

Sandown (Walks 1, 6) is the most northerly of the three major resorts on the east coast, set in the centre of 6-mile Sandown Bay behind a long sandy beach. As with Shanklin and Ventnor, the town started to thrive with the coming of the railway, and for about a century was the quintessential island resort for families wanting a bit of no-frills sun and fun. Since the decline of family tourism, however, the town has a slightly run-down feel even in summer, not having the charm of Shanklin or the magnificent location of Ventnor to sustain it. That said, it does boast the only surviving pleasure pier on the island, the bay's seascape from Culver Cliff to the southeast downs is enviable, and the town still makes a perfectly good, practical base for a walking holiday.

Despite being just 2 miles from Ryde, there is a distinctness and certain integrity about **Seaview** (Walks 2, 28), and it certainly feels a 'cut above' its westerly neighbour. Fine old houses abound, many of which today are seasonal second homes, and its residents include a large number of retirees. Development started in the early 1800s, and its crowning glory was a marvellous pier built in 1881 – one of only two in the country designed as a series of suspension bridges – but it was destroyed in a storm on Boxing Day 1950, a devastating event for village and island alike. Although Seaview is technically a resort, its charm lies in its upmarket status, so unlike its larger neighbours further south it does not court the masses.

Along with Sandown to the north and Ventnor to the south, **Shanklin** (Walks 6, 20, 21, 22, 23, 32) is one of the principal bases for visitors,

Sea wall to Ventnor (Walk 6)

offering an abundance of accommodation. It is indeed an ideal place to stay, with clean beaches, several independent shops, the quaint if rather vacuous Old Village, and a generally pleasant atmosphere. Like Sandown, transport links are frequent to both Ryde and Newport. The resort, including the Old Village, only really developed during the 19th century courtesy of the railway, and visitors – including Darwin, Dickens, Austen and Keats – flocked to rest on the beach, visit the dramatic Chine, taste the allegedly health-restoring spring water and (from 1890) visit the pier, sadly destroyed in the hurricane of 1987.

Shorwell (Walks 10, 11, 33) (pronounced 'shorall') and Brighstone are the principal villages on the Back of the Wight. While the latter is larger and closer to the coastline, the former has a humbler, more sheltered and introspective feel. Certainly it is photogenic, with the obligatory thatched stone cottages and charming medieval church (originally 12th century but almost rebuilt in the 15th). Less well known are Shorwell's secluded three manor houses, all dating from Tudor (West Court, Wolverton Manor) to early Stuart times (North Court). The village was extended somewhat in the 1980s, but its historic core has been left unmolested.

Surely to most eyes the classiest and most attractive of the island's three major seaside resorts, **Ventnor** (Walks 6, 7, 20, 27, 34), like Sandown and Shanklin, was little more than a fishing hamlet before the 19th century, centred around a mill and waterfall to the east of the modern town's promenade (the mill is long gone but 'the cascade' remains). The turning point came in 1829 when renowned physician Sir James Clark extolled the virtues of the climate and well-heeled mainlanders took notice. The 1840s especially saw great expansion and the building of three successive piers, the third being demolished in 1993 after fire damage. Another major boost came with the arrival of the railway from Ryde in 1866, and to a lesser extent a branch line from Merstone in 1900. Ventnor and its surrounding coastline are notoriously prone to landslip because of the vulnerable 'blue slipper' soft clay, and subsidence is a very real concern to property owners. But this vulnerability is more than offset by the sunny and mild microclimate: Churchill, Gandhi, Marx and Elgar are just some of the notables to have enjoyed it, and it makes the town the perfect location for the island's botanic gardens.

Yarmouth (Walks 4, 5, 13, 14) is one of the oldest towns on the island (reputedly also the smallest in the UK) and has quite a special ambience: graceful and immediately appealing. The town's origins go back to Saxon times, and it was mentioned in the *Domesday book* as 'Ermud' (muddy estuary), but the turning point came in 1135 when it received its charter. Trade increased, and King John made the town his personal headquarters twice in the early 13th century. Yarmouth managed to withstand 14th-century French raids (unlike nearby Newtown) but, as a precaution, 200 years later Yarmouth Castle was built by King Henry VIII, and can be visited today (English Heritage). Yarmouth is the destination port for ferries from Lymington and is the perfect starting point for some easy walking along the Coastal Path and beside the Western Yar.

TOP TEN ATTRACTIONS

If or when you fancy a break from walking, or the weather demands it, there are a number of recommended places to visit:

- **Osborne House** Queen Victoria and Prince Albert's holiday home is the most significant attraction on the island (search www.english-heritage.org.uk).
- **Carisbrooke Castle** (search www.english-heritage.org.uk).
- **Brading Roman Villa** (www.bradingromanvilla.org.uk). There is also a lesser-known Roman villa in Newport.
- **Isle of Wight Steam Railway** (www.iwsteamrailway.co.uk). Essential for Walk 26.
- **Dinosaur Isle**, Sandown (www.dinosaurisle.com).
- **Museum of Island History** (search www.iwight.com). Small, under-visited museum in Newport's Guildhall.
- **Dimbola Lodge** (www.dimbola.co.uk).

The Freshwater home of Victorian photographer Julia Margaret Cameron, often hosting some fine exhibitions.
- **Blackgang Chine amusement park** (www.blackgangchine.com). First opened its doors in 1843! Definitely more for young children, but also fun if you're young at heart.
- **Robin Hill Country Park** (www.robin-hill.com). Blackgang's younger sibling (both were started by the Dabell family).
- **Needles Park** (www.theneedles.co.uk). Take the famous chairlift down to Alum Bay.

There is a host of other smaller attractions too, so check out the relevant literature in print or online (see Appendix B).

WILDLIFE

The wide variety of plants and eco-systems found on the island can be attributed not only to its diverse range of landscape – including woodland, downs, wide estuaries, tidal creeks, marshland and large protected nature reserves, such as Brading Marshes – but also to a year-round temperate climate.

Especially in the northeast, the island is filled with rich mixed woodland, much of it ancient. Previous policies of coniferous planting which, it was assumed, would assist the red

Western Yar, with Freshwater Church in the background (Walk 14)

squirrel population are now being overturned, and the trend is now for more planting of native (deciduous) species. Plants unique (or almost) to the island include Martin's ramping-fumitory, early gentian, field cow-wheat, and the exceptionally rare wood calamint. 27 distinct species of orchid can also be found.

In terms of animal life, the island is special not just for its renowned red squirrel population, but also for dormice, which are common in much of the island's woodland. The island is also a great place to see birds, with notable numbers of wintering species such as Brent geese, teal and widgeon, which complement other species commonly seen on the island such as the magnificent peregrine falcon, nightjars, woodcocks, long-eared owls, firecrests,

cormorants, shags and, of course, gulls. It is also one of the few places left in the country where the beautiful wasp-coloured Granville fritillary butterfly can be seen hovering around the sea cliffs (one of several butterfly species). Newtown Harbour is a particularly special place for birdwatching; a bird hide has been built for that purpose, where sightings are recorded.

The island also has a number of wildlife-related tourist attractions such as Seaview Wildlife Encounter, Owl and Monkey Haven, Amazon World and Butterfly World, as well as the larger Isle of Wight Zoo based in Sandown and Ventnor Botanic Garden. The Garden has recently introduced wall lizards, the largest UK colony of which exists in the wild between it and the town centre.

WHEN TO GO

The wonderful thing about the Isle of Wight is that the climate is conducive to walking at any time of year. Winters are generally milder than in most places in the UK and snow is a rare event, even on higher ground. Conversely, summer temperatures tend to be lower than most of the south of England, with a refreshing breeze, so there are not many days when it is too hot to walk. Rainfall is about average for southern England – so unlikely to be a significant issue. And last but not least, the island is a suntrap: Shanklin is widely regarded as one of the sunniest places in the UK, and neighbouring Ventnor has its own warm and sunny microclimate.

As well as the benefits of lower accommodation prices and fewer tourists, winter tends to complement walks by the sea, and a week spent walking the Coastal Path in the colder months is recommended, especially for hardier walkers. There are usually numerous pubs to warm you up, and buses generally run to the same time-table year round. For bad-weather days, many of the larger attractions remain open throughout the year.

The season really gets going from early April: tourist numbers and accommodation prices increase, although even in the height of summer the island seldom feels crowded and the pace stays relaxed. May brings beautiful fields of fragrant rapeseed and wildflowers, and summer and autumn are perfect for exploring the island's scattered forests and woodland. From the end of October, when the trees are shedding their leaves and visitors start to leave, walkers in the know continue to explore and appreciate the island.

Path up to the Long Stone (Walk 13)

Southampton–Cowes catamaran

GETTING TO THE ISLAND

The idea of a bridge across the Solent is periodically mooted locally, as the mainland is just a few miles away, but there is much opposition to this idea from many islanders for practical, ideological and aesthetic reasons.

Therefore, as has been the case for thousands of years, the only way to get to the island is by sea. **Car-ferry services** can also be used by foot passengers (see the first table below).

The second table shows the services that are for **foot passengers** only.

Car-ferry services (can also be used by foot passengers)

Mainland	Island	Journey time	Operator
Portsmouth Harbour	Fishbourne (near Ryde)	40mins	Wightlink
Southampton Town Quay	East Cowes	1hr	Red Funnel
Lymington Pier	Yarmouth	35mins	Wightlink

Ferry services (foot passengers only)

Mainland	Island	Journey time	Seacraft	Operator
Portsmouth Harbour station	Ryde Pier	20mins	Catamaran	Wightlink
Southsea (Clarence Pier)	Ryde Esplanade	10mins	Hovercraft	Hovertravel
Southampton Town Quay	(West) Cowes	25mins	Catamaran	Red Funnel

Southsea–Ryde hovercraft

The above services vary in frequency from every 15mins to every 90mins; timetables can be easily accessed online. Tickets for car and foot passengers can be bought both in advance and at the port, and there are frequently special offers available, so look at the operators' websites before purchasing (see Appendix B).

Through train/ferry tickets can be bought to any station on the Island Line (between Ryde Pier and Shanklin), and to Cowes, East Cowes and Yarmouth.

Needles Breezer bus at the New Battery (Walk 9)

GETTING AROUND

The island's road network is good, yet traffic is noticeably light, and driving along the many rural roads and country lanes can be delightful. Many of the walks in this book are suitable for drivers, being either circular or involving no more than a short bus journey from the finish back to your car. Parking is often free or low cost, and details are provided for each walk.

Taking a car onto the ferry can be expensive, however, so you may wish to consider leaving it on the mainland. The island's bus service, operated by Southern Vectis, is excellent: comprehensive, fast and usually extremely reliable. All the walks in this book are accessible by bus, and a journey across the island from Ryde or Sandown to Alum Bay takes only about 90mins. Before heading out on a walk make sure that you obtain one of Southern Vectis' user-friendly bus timetables, available at Newport, Yarmouth and Ryde bus stations and from the Southern Vectis website (www.islandbuses. info). They show all the bus routes on the island and are an essential navigation aid (the website also provides a detailed network map – go to *route maps* then click on *network map*). In summary the main routes are as follows.

Route	Recommended use between	Current daily frequency
1	Newport–Cowes	Usually 6–8 per hour
2	Newport–Shanklin/Sandown Ryde–Shanklin/Godshill	2 per hour
3	Newport–Ventnor Ryde–Shanklin	2 per hour
4	Ryde–East Cowes	1 per hour
5	Newport–East Cowes	3 per hour Mon–Sat 2 per hour Sundays
6	Newport–Niton Ventnor–Niton/Chale	1 per hour Mon–Sat (route varies between Ventnor and Niton). 4 journeys Sundays
7	Newport–Alum Bay	2 per hour
8	Newport–Sandown Ryde–Bembridge	1 per hour
9	Newport–Ryde	6 per hour Mon–Sat 4 per hour Sundays
12	Newport–Freshwater Bay	4–6 journeys per day

Appuldurcombe House (Walk 32)

Single and return tickets can be bought on any bus to any destination on the island, even if you need to change buses, but daily or longer bus passes provide best value.

Open-top buses complement the usual routes in season, and a trip on at least one of these is highly recommended. These trips are currently included in the price of bus passes, and as they are hop-on-hop-off services they can be used as conventional buses. The routes currently in operation are the Needles Breezer (a circuit from Yarmouth via Freshwater Bay and the Needles) and the Downs Breezer (a circuit from Ryde taking in Robin Hill Adventure Park, Amazon World and Ashey Down).

There is also a seasonal Island Coaster service running clockwise from Ryde to Yarmouth every morning and returning from Alum Bay every afternoon. This can be especially handy for travelling between one of the eastern resorts and the Back of the Wight. Again, bus passes are currently valid on this service.

A useful train service (officially called the Island Line) runs between Ryde Pier and Shanklin, a relic of the many steam railway lines which once criss-crossed the island. A quirk is that the trains are 1930s London Underground stock, which is often a source of amusement for visitors stepping off the Portsmouth catamaran. Trains are generally every 30mins, timed to connect with the catamaran.

ACCOMMODATION

Most visitors stay in one of the seaside resorts on the east of the island: Sandown, Shanklin or Ventnor. Hotels and B&Bs for all budgets are ubiquitous in the three places. Sandown generally offers the lowest rates and Ventnor the highest, with prices varying according to season but 'mini-peaking' over Christmas and New Year. Websites like Tripadvisor are handy to find the most popular places, but there are no significant concerns over standards.

While the resorts certainly make excellent choices for a walking break, there are less conventional alternatives. Interesting and often upmarket places can be found in areas such as Seaview, Niton Undercliff and Mottistone; and cottages, camping and other self-catering options can be found all over the island, sometimes in pleasingly remote locations. Newport has budget chain hotels and a few boutique hotels, and makes a good base for travellers relying on public transport who wish to visit the whole island and prefer the bustle of a town to staying by the sea. Ryde and Cowes also offer a sprinkling of accommodation.

For those on a strict budget, there are Youth Hostel Association hostels in Totland (open throughout the year) and Brighstone (summer holiday only).

USING THIS GUIDE

The 34 walks in this book could keep the walker occupied for weeks. Each and every route offers a unique

Brighstone Forest (Walk 19)

experience, and is worth doing both for its own sake and to add to one's appreciation of the island's diversity. This emphasis on quality has meant that many of the council's official trails are not included because, curiously, they don't quite cut the mustard.

The walks begin with the Coastal Path along the north coast (Walks 1–5) and the south coast (Walks 6–9). These are described in what I view as the best walking directions – from east to west – not as a purely circular route. This is followed by walks in West Wight (Walks 10–19) and East Wight (Walks 20–34). Ranging from 6.5km (4.1 miles) to 26km (16 miles), the routes explore not only popular areas such as around the Needles and along the Coastal Path, but also parts of the island which are less well known to visitors, such as Parkhurst Forest, Ashey and Mersley Downs, and the Niton Undercliff. Except in the height of summer you should encounter few other walkers, especially on the lesser-known paths, and indeed one of the advantages of walking here is the peace and quiet that it brings.

Footpaths are generally in very good order across the island, although care is needed after heavy rain, especially off the high ground. Waymarking is generally good; all official footpaths and bridleways have a unique reference based on the parish in which they are located – so, for example, footpath F14 is located in Freshwater – and these are almost always included on signposts. The council's official trails, such as the Coastal Path and Tennyson Trail, are named on signposts only sporadically, and following the trails using these signposts alone would be difficult.

All walks are accessible by public transport: to the start, from the finish, and often from at least somewhere in between. One of the top priorities in compiling this book has been accuracy: each walk has been carefully checked to ensure that descriptions are clear and unambiguous, and that route-finding is as straightforward as possible.

All abilities are catered for, with some of the easier walks being appropriate for older people and children (see 'Walking with children' below). At the other end of the scale, the interconnectedness of many walks may lead hardy walkers to do two or three in one day.

Information is provided at the start of every walk description about its distance, difficulty grade, required walking time, refreshment facilities, access to the start and from the finish by public transport, where to park and opportunities to finish early. Walking time estimates are deliberately generous to allow for slower walkers, but they assume continuous walking – so factor in time for lunch and random stops. 'Grade' refers mainly to the level of fitness needed to complete the walk, irrespective of length. So a long but mainly flat walk would be graded 'easy', whereas a short and very hilly walk would be graded 'strenuous'.

To a lesser extent, factors such as ease of route-finding and condition of the terrain may also be taken into consideration.

In the route description, key places along the route appear in **bold** to help with navigation. Ordnance Survey mapping is included for each walk with the route clearly marked.

WHAT TO TAKE

What to take on a walk depends largely on your disposition, but every walker should always take the following essentials.

- **Weather-appropriate clothing** Remember to check the forecast for the whole day and be prepared for all reasonable eventualities. More breathable fabrics will aid your comfort.
- **Lightweight walking boots** will be needed for most walks even on dry days, so should be regarded as essential. After rain, boots are essential on every walk.
- **Food and water** in inverse proportion to availability of refreshment retailers (and more than you think you need)
- **Suncream**, **sunglasses** and a **sunhat** when necessary
- Basic **first-aid kit**

For longer walks or in more remote areas, it may prudent to bring a mobile phone (although coverage can be patchy), map, compass and emergency torch and/or whistle, especially if walking alone. The 1:25,000

Ordnance Survey map for the Isle of Wight (Explorer sheet OL29) – smaller scale than the map used for this book – would also be a good investment, and a pedometer might assist in following directions. Finally, knowledge of tide times may assist with some walks (see website in Appendix B).

SAFETY

A great advantage of walking on the island is that it is possible to enjoy magnificent scenery without seriously losing your way, and the chances of encountering any nasty accidents are slim. But if a problem were to occur, habitation and medical facilities would never be far away (there is an A&E department at St Mary's Hospital in Newport).

Keep an eye on the weather as high winds – which can occur frequently – can cause difficulties both on the downs and along the coast. An entirely windless day, sunny or cloudy, often makes walking on the island idyllic, but the obvious tip on

Crossing the steam railway (Walk 29)

windy days is to choose a walk following the wind's direction. And if the forecast looks dubious choose a walk which has a possibility of finishing early. Finally, with respect to weather, don't walk on the downs when mist or fog is forecast, and treat cliff-tops with respect.

Insects can be a minor nuisance in the warmer months, but the island is not significantly affected by ticks, which are becoming more common in the UK and can carry Lyme Disease. You may wish to take precautions, however. Curious cows may also be about on some of the walks, which can be a bit unnerving at first, but just ignore them and they'll lose interest.

Finally, take care not to over-exert yourself, especially on remote walks that can't easily be shortened.

THE COUNTRYSIDE

The island is a beautiful place, so do try to keep it that way. The fundamental principle is to leave no trace of your visit except your goodwill to the people you meet!

You should use common sense if straying off footpaths, even though the CROW Act (2000) provides the walker with the freedom to walk off-path in certain areas, such as downland and coastal areas, irrespective of whether they are privately owned. Such open access areas are often indicated on the island (and elsewhere) by signs showing a brown, circular symbol with a person walking, and are also marked on Ordnance Survey Explorer maps.

WALKING IN GROUPS

If you are walking with even just one other person, remember that walking speeds and abilities vary, and that the sensible (and polite) thing to do is to choose a walk which can be accomplished by the least able person in the group and pace it to the slowest.

WALKING WITH CHILDREN

The island is well known as a family destination, and some of the walks in this book would be suitable for children. Indulging in a few walks could definitely enhance a family holiday, and the introductory information for each walk will help parents decide which might be appropriate. Two very easy hikes for all the family to enjoy are the Coastal Path stretches from Seaview to Ryde – passing the playground at Puckpool Park – and Sandown to Shanklin (Walks 2 and 6 respectively). Particular care should, of course, be taken near cliff edges.

COASTAL PATH

St Lawrence coastline (Walk 7)

Cliffs near Ventnor (Walk 7)

If recreational walking is the island's crown, then the Coastal Path of about 70 miles must be its jewel. The path circumnavigates the island, and throughout its length offers ever-changing scenic variety. Compare for instance the wildness of the Back of the Wight to the very tame stretch between Sandown and Shanklin, or the sheer drama of the far south and far west sections with the gentle inland meanderings between Cowes and Yarmouth. Every stage of the Coastal Path is worth doing in order to appreciate the sheer diversity of the island's coastline.

The Path is presented here in nine approximately day-long stages and, unusually, as a route in two parts: from Sandown in the east to Alum Bay in the west along both coasts – north (Walks 1–5) and south (Walks 6–9). Walking the Path in this way (rather than as a circuit) greatly enhances the experience by revealing the best of the island's views: for instance, walking from Sandown to Chale (south-coast route) is more exciting than vice-versa, yet the section from Yarmouth to Alum Bay (north-coast route) cries out to be walked in that direction, as the approach to the Needles both prior to and from the top of Headon Warren is magnificent.

Fast and frequent bus services and lack of accommodation options in the more remote west of the island are additional reasons why the Coastal Path should be viewed as a series of day walks rather than as a continuous loop. However, walkers who want to undertake the Coastal Path as a circuit could easily do so by following a combination of these directions in reverse and signposts.

Due to the ever-present problems of erosion and landslips, there may be diversions in place on some short stretches.

NORTH COAST

WALK 1
Sandown to Bembridge Point

Start	Sandown Pier
Finish	Bembridge Point
Distance	9.8km (6.1 miles)
Grade	Moderate
Time	3½hrs
Refreshments	Lord Yarborough Monument (3.5km), Bembridge (6.5km)
Public transport	*To start* Bus routes 2, 3 and 8, and train (the pier is a 10mins walk from the station); *from finish* Bus route 8
Parking	Sandown Esplanade
Early finish	Bembridge (6.3km, bus route 8)

This stage of the Coastal Path leads out of the popular resort of Sandown and up onto the sea cliffs of Bembridge Down, aiming for the Lord Yarborough Monument at the top and offering sweeping views of Sandown Bay behind. Take the opportunity to enjoy northerly views from the monument before descending gradually to magnificent Whitecliff Bay to pick up a wooded path to the outskirts of Bembridge. You may wish to rest at the Victorian Crab and Lobster Inn before following a sea wall and footpaths round to Bembridge Point at the start of Bembridge Harbour. Note that good walking boots will be needed for this walk because short stretches near the former Bembridge School can be exceptionally muddy.

Facing the pier at **Sandown** (accommodation, super-markets, pubs, cafés, restaurants, shops, toilets) turn left, walking along the promenade or beach. At the end of **Yaverland** car park, continue on the grass following the signpost, always aiming for the Lord Yarborough Monument on the cliffs ahead. In terms of fossil-spotting, the beach at Yaverland is second only to Compton Bay. As

Yaverland cliffs

the route ascends, don't forget to look back to Sandown Bay and the downs beyond: a memorable view and ever more majestic the higher you rise.

Sandown Pier is the only functioning pleasure pier on the island. Looking at its rather subdued state today, it is hard to believe that in its heyday it hosted such distinguished guests as the Queen and

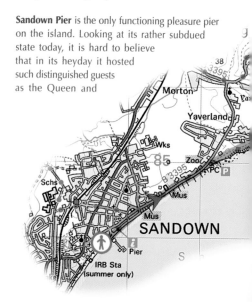

Lord Mountbatten (penultimate island Governor), and entertainers including Harry Secombe, Bob Monkhouse and Lenny Henry, as well as providing ferry services to Portsmouth. The pier was built in 1876 and subsequently much refurbished. Entertainment was provided at a pavilion at the shore-end of the pier: before being reconstructed in 1968, it boasted an incredible 980 seats.

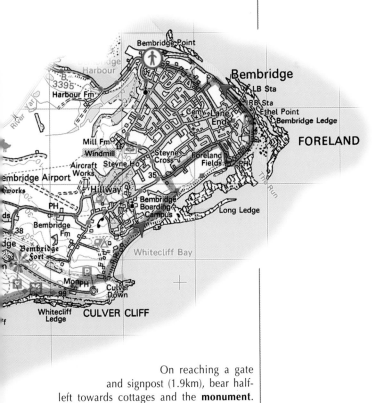

On reaching a gate and signpost (1.9km), bear half-left towards cottages and the **monument**. The weather can be tempestuous up here – as on all exposed high ground on the island – but on a clear day the view from the monument stretches beyond Bembridge Airport and Harbour, over the Spithead to and beyond Portsmouth. Savour the moment and keep an eye out for light aircraft landing.

Erected in 1849, the 104m (341ft) **Lord Yarborough Monument** commemorates the memory of Charles Anderson-Pelham, 1st Earl of Yarborough, Lincolnshire MP, and island notable by virtue of being the first Commodore of Cowes' Royal Yacht Squadron, marrying into the Worsley family, and

Lord Yarborough Monument

consequently coming to own Appuldurcombe House. The monument was originally placed where Bembridge Fort is now, but was relocated here on construction of the latter.

Descend half-right (no path) towards the holiday park, turning full right just before the descent becomes too steep. Just before a gate bear left downhill. Ignore ways off and, emerging from bushes (250m), bear sharp right, continuing to follow the coastline. Look out for the Coastal Path sign (90m) and continue, with beautiful **Whitecliff Bay** to your right. Its magnificent beach soon comes into view.

At the end of the holiday park, with benches opposite, bear right then turn left at a junction of paths to keep following the coastline, now in woodland. Ignore ways off; after over 1km the path swings left past a Coastal Path diversion sign and emerges onto a road. Turn right, now entering **Bembridge** (limited accommodation, supermarket, pubs, cafés, restaurants, shops, toilets). ▶ After a further 200m bear right to rejoin the original Coastal Path by the Crab and Lobster, where a beer may not go amiss.

Descend the steps to the right of the inn and turn left to walk along the sea wall. Where the wall ends, deviate from the official route by continuing on the beach around Bembridge **Foreland**, the eastern vertex of the island. Walk up the steps shortly before the RNLI pier and continue past the RNLI shop along the sea wall (or beach). ▶

At the end of the wall ascend steps and at the end of the path bear left. Follow the signposted footpath in 200m and ignore all ways off until after 550m, then turn right on another signposted footpath, reaching a road near **Bembridge Point** with the bus stops beyond. To detour to the Point itself (recommended) continue to the end of Beach Road opposite the pub.

To shorten the walk turn left along a footpath after 550m, keeping straight on at the road, to reach a bus stop serving both directions.

The Bembridge Lifeboat Station was established in 1867. It currently has two lifeboats and is open daily to visitors.

WALK 2
Bembridge Point to Ryde

Start	Bembridge Point (Toll Gate café)
Finish	Ryde Esplanade
Distance	9.3km (5.8 miles)
Grade	Moderate, on account of the very muddy middle section
Time	3hrs
Refreshments	Seaview (5.7km), Spring Vale (7km), Appley (seasonal, 8.1km)
Public transport	*To start* Bus route 8; *from finish* Bus routes 2, 3, 4, 8 and 9, and train
Parking	Car park at the western end of the harbour road
Early finish	Seaview (5.8km, bus route 8)

There is 1km of road walking at the start of this stretch of the Coastal Path, but it is far from dull as Bembridge Harbour is there to entertain you. A narrow causeway leads over often flooded marshland from the harbour to St Helens Duver – site of the island's first golf course – and the evocative tower of St Helens Old Church, completely incongruous with its surroundings. From here the walk deviates from the official Coastal Path by exploring sublime Priory Bay and the little-used wooded paths just above it. Priory Bay leads into Seagrove Bay and the start of Seaview, a low-key seaside village with many intriguing houses. The route then continues along the shoreline to Ryde, with frequent views over the Spithead to the mainland.

For facilities at Bembridge, see Walk 1.

◀ First, make the short detour to **Bembridge Point** 'proper'. Walk past the fountain near the bus stops and turn left into Beach Road – the reward is a 180° sea view at the end, with St Helens Fort facing you.

An outing is arranged every summer, when the tide is particularly low, to view the Victorian **St Helens Fort** from St Helens Old Church, here visible as a white structure to the left. Other Spithead forts are seen during the walk. They were built as defences in

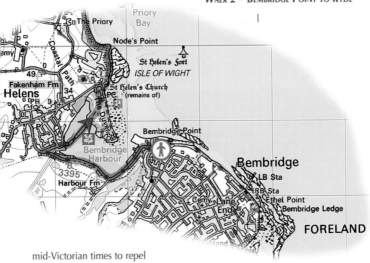

mid-Victorian times to repel
a French invasion that never came,
and have become known as Palmerston Forts (or
Follies) after the relevant Prime Minister.

Map continues on
page 49

Back on the 'main' road, walk southwest, with
Bembridge Harbour on the right. A few boats have been
converted into idiosyncratic B&Bs. Cross the Eastern Yar
(1.3km) and take the first right (Latimer Road). Keep to
this direction until the sea wall, which becomes a delightful causeway above the marshland. It is possible that you
will have just the seabirds for company!

Bembridge Harbour has been in use since pre-
Roman times and originally penetrated southwest
as far as Brading, the enlarged body of water being
known as Brading Harbour or Brading Haven. The
water was drained from the southwest part of the
harbour in 1388 leaving mudflats, which were in
turn reclaimed from the sea as late as 1878, eventually becoming today's Brading Marshes Nature
Reserve. The resultant embankment provided a
new route between Bembridge and St Helens and

45

also played host to the Brading to Bembridge railway branch line which operated from 1882 to 1953. It was from the harbour that Edward III set sail to invade Normandy in 1346, and it is said that it was the last stop for Nelson and his crew en route to the Battle of Trafalgar in 1805.

At the end of the causeway bear half-left on a faint path. You are now on **St Helens Duver**.

Duver is an island term for sand dune, and these former dunes, now National Trust land, were developed into the island's first golf course, at one time internationally renowned and played on by royalty and other distinguished visitors. The marsh and scrub here host a wide variety of plant life.

Aim for the pillared Old Club House to the left – now a National Trust holiday cottage. At the junction a little further on, the official route continues on the footpath opposite, but this walk turns right towards the tower of St Helens Old Church, rather incongruously placed between attractive beaches on both sides.

St Helens Causeway

46

St Helens Old Church is a characterful old relic right on the seafront. The tower is all that remains of a 13th-century church that started disintegrating, and fell out of use, in Tudor times. In 1703 it was bricked up, and some years later was replaced by a new church further inland. Today it has no practical importance other than its white seaward side serving as an unusual seamark.

St Helens Old Church

Turn left to start an exploration of **Priory Bay**. Walkers who are sure-footed over rocks and aware of the tide times might be able to walk all the way to Seaview along the beach, but do not attempt this if you are not completely confident about the tide and your abilities. The recommended route is to walk along the beach almost as far as the rocks at the end. Ascend steps to join a lovely, wooded but little-known sea path, shortly ascending and descending more steps. The trees, birdsong and wide secluded beach ahead can (somewhat) give the impression that you're in the tropics. Certainly a contrast to the start of the walk! But every rose has its thorn – in this case thick mud, so be careful.

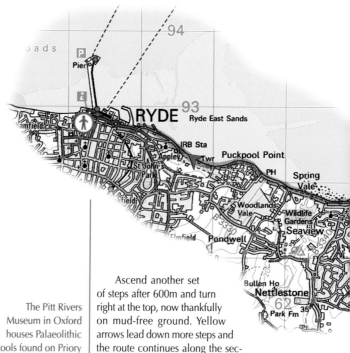

The Pitt Rivers Museum in Oxford houses Palaeolithic tools found on Priory Bay Beach which could be up to 700,000 years old.

Ascend another set of steps after 600m and turn right at the top, now thankfully on mud-free ground. Yellow arrows lead down more steps and the route continues along the section of Priory Bay Beach glimpsed earlier – technically private for guests of the nearby hotel, but it is a public right of way. ◄

At the end of the beach turn left up steps and shortly descend again towards **Seagrove Bay** and its colourful waterfront houses. When obliged to turn inland, immediately follow footpath R105, now having rejoined the official Coastal Path. Walk behind the waterfront houses seen earlier, all of which look unique and very intriguing. Bear right at the end of the row to return to the shoreline.

A very striking and unusual **pier** consisting of three suspension bridges stood here from 1881 to 1951 (when, devastatingly, it was destroyed by a storm).

It hosted ferries from Portsmouth and was complemented by a large hotel, a site now occupied by a block of flats with an original and tasteful design.

Ascend into the village of **Seaview** (pub, cafés, restaurants, shops, toilets), which provides the opportunity to find some refreshments. Turn right at the crossroads down the high street to return to the shore – or to end the walk continue to the T-junction and turn left for the bus stops.

Look out for R91 at the end of the esplanade. Once on it, the route stays by the shoreline all the way to Ryde. The 5mins saunter round Hersey Nature Reserve (450m) makes a pleasant detour. Between Oakhill Road and the Boat House pub is a 'suburb' of Seaview called **Spring Vale**. Past the Boat House there is a choice of paths: through the centre of Puckpool Park ahead (converted from a battery in 1928) or either of the parallel shoreside paths. Beyond Puckpool the walk enters the once private Appley Towers Estate, now pleasant parkland.

Striking shoreside folly **Appley Tower** was erected in 1875 and used as a 'tea room' for King George V and Queen Mary during their visits to owner Sir Hedworth Williamson.

Continue into **Ryde** (accommodation, supermarkets, pubs, cafés, restaurants, shops, toilets), reaching the pier and public transport in about 30mins. Look out for the hovercraft whizzing across the Solent.

49

WALK 3

Ryde to Cowes

Start	Ryde Pier
Finish	East Cowes or Cowes
Distance	12.1km (7.6 miles)
Grade	Fairly easy
Time	4hrs
Refreshments	Quarr Abbey (3.3km), Fishbourne (4.1km), Wootton Bridge (5.5km)
Public transport	*To start* Bus routes 2, 3, 4, 8 and 9, and train; *from East Cowes* Bus routes 4 and 5
Parking	Long-stay car parks in St Thomas Street, just west of the pier
Early finish	Fishbourne (5km, bus routes 4 and 9), Whippingham (9.3km, bus routes 4 and 5). At no point is the route further than 20mins from the main road (with bus stops).

Although there is a fair amount of road walking in this section, and the route doesn't follow the coast as closely as other Coastal Path sections (indeed, the Solent is rarely even to be seen on this stretch), this is surprisingly a mostly pretty walk, often among trees and with plenty of birdsong for company. The roads are mainly minor and quiet, usually with good views, and the walk deviates favourably from the official route by visiting Whippingham Church, with its memorable view of the Medina from the churchyard, and by staying close to the river all the way into East Cowes. Finally, the little-known but magnificent Quarr Abbey features early on: its church is considered one of the finest modern ecclesiastical buildings in Europe, and its peaceful gardens make a wonderful spot for a picnic lunch.

Facing the pier at **Ryde** (accommodation, supermarkets, pubs, cafés, restaurants, shops, toilets) turn left along the esplanade. Note the elegant, colonnaded Prince Consort Building: built in 1846 as a gift from Prince Albert to Queen Victoria, it was originally the home of the Royal Victoria Yacht Club, founded because the Royal Yacht Squadron at Cowes didn't allow female members. Once

Map continues on
page 53

back on the road, turn right. Take the first right into narrow
Buckingham Road, shortly bearing left and turning right at
the top. Continue along this quiet road until virtually at the
main road, then turn right onto a signposted footpath, with
Ryde golf course to the right and left.

Reach Binstead Church, turn left with the road,
then bear right past a very picturesque thatched cottage. Shortly afterwards turn right to follow an earth
road – not the footpath beside it – and right again at the
T-junction. Ignore ways off to pass the ruins of **Old Quarr
Abbey** after 450m. At a crossroads after a further 300m,
detour right to see the 'modern' red-brick **Quarr Abbey**,
somewhat incongruous in its tame surroundings. Both
the abbey and its grounds are well worth exploring and,
being under-publicised, tourists are few and far between.
Refreshments may be had at the tea shop, if it is open,
and the gardens make a perfect picnic spot.

The present **Quarr Abbey** (pronounced 'cor') is
so named because of an important nearby quarry
mined since Roman times, which provided materi-
als to build Winchester and Chichester cathedrals,
and Winchester College. It was completed in 1912
to house a French Benedictine order, persecuted in
their own country, which had moved to but subsequently outgrown Appuldurcombe House. Many of
the original monks returned to France in 1922 and
English monks moved in, but it took a further 15
years for the abbey to become independent. It is
today still actively used and maintained by about

51

Quarr Abbey

10 Benedictine followers. Check out the very comprehensive website (**www.quarrabbey.co.uk**).

To the east are the ruins of a **Cistercian abbey** constructed from 1132 and demolished in 1536 during the dissolution of the monasteries. In its heyday it was the foremost religious institution on the island and apparently served as a prison for Henry II's queen, Eleanor.

Return to the crossroads and continue in the previous direction. Ignoring ways off, emerge opposite the **Fishbourne Inn** and turn left. Pass Fishbourne ferry terminal, and 200m further turn right on footpath R1 and left at the T-junction, now with occasional views towards Wootton Creek. Where the lane swings left go straight ahead on a track marked 'The Plantation'. Ascend to the main road and there turn right beside the bus stop for Ryde (the stop for Newport is a little further). Cross Wootton Bridge, between Old Mill Pond, which can look idyllic in the right light, and the marina on Wootton Creek, into the village of **Wootton Bridge** (supermarket, pubs, restaurants, shops, toilets).

Wootton Creek has been in use since pre-Roman times, and there has been a crossing here also since time immemorial. It was this crossing that spawned the settlement of Wootton Bridge, which had traditionally been separate from Wootton further up the hill. Only recently have the two amalgamated to the extent that the names are often used interchangeably. Wootton was also the site of the 1969 Isle of Wight Festival, featuring Bob Dylan.

Immediately over the bridge, bear right past the Sloop Inn. Where the track swings right, continue along a passageway and turn right at the road. Turn left on N97 (70m) keeping ahead in another 70m, soon on a passageway between houses. Then at a road junction turn left. Turn left into another passageway after 50m; continue over the grass soon ahead and into Footways opposite. Turn left at the end then immediately right into Brocks Copse Road – thankfully it's a lovely quiet lane after the bungalows peter out, as it is yours for over 2km!

On eventually reaching the main road at **Whippingham** (small post office – limited opening – with basic groceries)

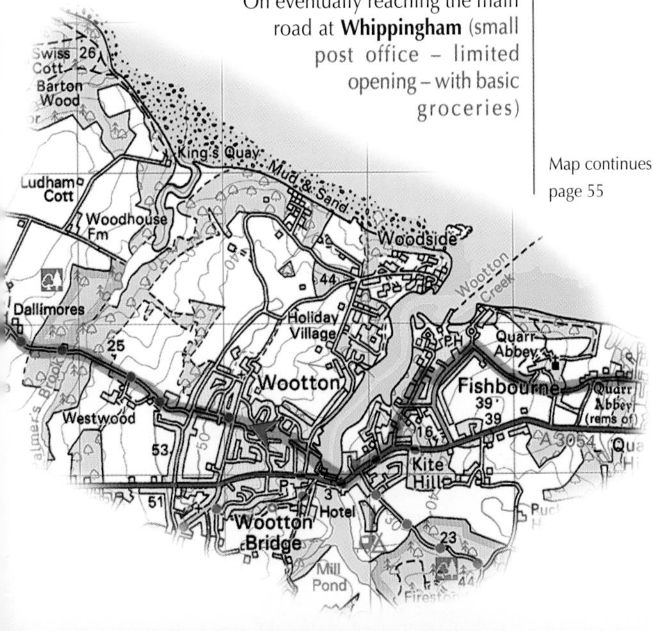

Map continues on page 55

53

turn right. The official Coastal Path simply follows this main road via Osborne House all the way to East Cowes but, unless you wish to visit Osborne today, the quieter and more interesting route is as follows. Pass bus stops and turn left almost immediately into Beatrice Avenue (named after Queen Victoria's daughter) and follow it to reach the Gothic-influenced tower and spires of Whippingham Church and almshouses opposite: at the back of the churchyard there is a lovely view of the Medina as well as potentially handy public toilets.

> **Whippingham Church** was Queen Victoria and Prince Albert's local church during their stays at Osborne House. Their daughter Beatrice was married and is buried here, as is the father of Philip, Duke of Edinburgh. The early medieval church was rebuilt twice, first in 1804 by famous architect and local John Nash (who went on to design London's Regent Street and Regent's Park), and then in 1854 a much larger church was designed, at least in part by Prince Albert, to accommodate the Queen's entourage; Albert's influence may account for the rather Germanic-looking exterior. Royal memorials abound in the Royal Pew, Battenburg Chapel and churchyard. The almshouses opposite the church were built on Queen Victoria's orders, in 1876, for retired royal servants, and apparently the Queen used to meet with parishioners there after church.

Continue along the road, shortly taking a path parallel to it. On reaching the row of multi-coloured houses continue along Monks Walk/Beatrice Avenue for a further 550m. Then, opposite Meadow Road, descend a footpath and keep ahead towards the river before eventually being obliged to turn right.

Just past East Cowes **cemetery**, it's worth detouring down Medina View for, as you might expect, a view of Cowes Marina and its hotchpotch of boats. Turn left at the T-junction ahead and follow this road to the centre of **East Cowes** (limited accommodation, supermarkets, pubs,

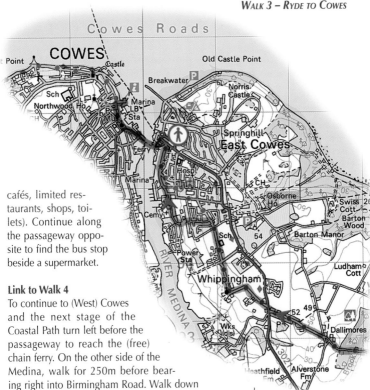

cafés, limited restaurants, shops, toilets). Continue along the passageway opposite to find the bus stop beside a supermarket.

Link to Walk 4

To continue to (West) Cowes and the next stage of the Coastal Path turn left before the passageway to reach the (free) chain ferry. On the other side of the Medina, walk for 250m before bearing right into Birmingham Road. Walk down Shooters Hill, which becomes the high street. At the Fountain Hotel, turn right down Town Quay for the Red Jet terminal, which is the start of Walk 4.

Cowes chain ferry

WALK 4
Cowes to Yarmouth

Start	Cowes Red Jet terminal
Finish	Yarmouth
Distance	24km (15 miles)
Grade	Easy
Time	9hrs
Refreshments	Gurnard (2.2km and 3km), Thorness Bay Holiday Park (6km), Porchfield (7.9km), Shalfleet (12.7km)
Public transport	*To start* Bus route 1 (or routes 4, 5 and 9 to East Cowes, transferring by chain ferry); *from finish* Bus route 7. **Tip** In season, bus route 21 runs twice in the late afternoon to Newport via Calbourne. The buses are open-top and hugely enjoyable in fine weather. The service is under-publicised and under-used. **Note** 'Mainlanders' could consider taking the Southampton to Cowes ferry and returning to Lymington from Yarmouth, but it would be an extremely long day.
Parking	Brunswick Road long-stay car park, near the chain ferry
Early finish	Gurnard (2.5km, bus route 32), Shalfleet (12.7km, bus route 7), Bouldnor (22.5km, bus route 7)

As with Walk 3, a substantial part of this Coastal Path section is inland because of the wide expanse of Newtown Harbour midway and a military zone just to its east. Nonetheless it is a walk of great variety and, particularly after Shalfleet, great beauty. From Cowes a long stretch along the seafront is followed by inland fields and a deviation from the official route from Porchfield to minimise roadwalking. After flirting with the once-bustling former port of Newtown, the route arrives at the village of Shalfleet, the perfect place to split this long walk if so inclined. Beyond, remote woodland, isolated farms and hamlets, and a deserted stony beach all beckon – this is one of the most tranquil and aesthetically pleasing parts of the island, especially in summer. The seclusion continues as the walk meanders through Bouldnor Forest and ends only shortly before Yarmouth. A sea wall and stroll down Yarmouth's attractive high street ends this wonderful walk.

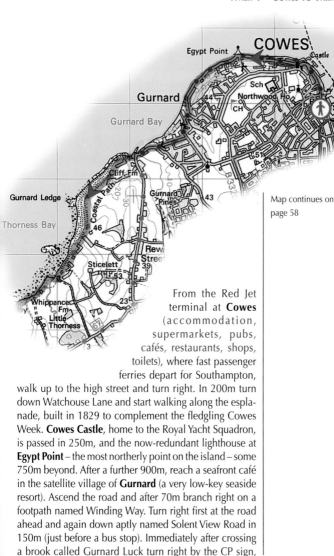

Map continues on page 58

From the Red Jet terminal at **Cowes** (accommodation, supermarkets, pubs, cafés, restaurants, shops, toilets), where fast passenger ferries depart for Southampton, walk up to the high street and turn right. In 200m turn down Watchouse Lane and start walking along the esplanade, built in 1829 to complement the fledgling Cowes Week. **Cowes Castle**, home to the Royal Yacht Squadron, is passed in 250m, and the now-redundant lighthouse at **Egypt Point** – the most northerly point on the island – some 750m beyond. After a further 900m, reach a seafront café in the satellite village of **Gurnard** (a very low-key seaside resort). Ascend the road and after 70m branch right on a footpath named Winding Way. Turn right first at the road ahead and again down aptly named Solent View Road in 150m (just before a bus stop). Immediately after crossing a brook called Gurnard Luck turn right by the CP sign,

57

Map continues on
page 61

shortly starting
to ascend.

Sea views on
the right soon give way to
country views on the left, and fur-
ther still you emerge out into the open with a sweeping
view of **Thorness Bay** and, in clear conditions, over to
the mainland's Hurst Beach (not, as it appears, part of the
island). Stay on the main path, descending gradually to
the beach at the bay. Continue along the beach, and in
500m turn left up a wide track, the grassy area making a
lovely spot for a picnic. This is the last time you will be by
the sea for a good few miles!

Walk up to a **holiday park**; bear left by its bar/restau-
rant then half-left onto a drive by the shop (past the no-
entry sign). At the next T-junction – facing holiday home
34 – go right. Very shortly turn right on a signposted
footpath, and after 60m bear left over a ditch. Turn left
at a T-junction and in 100m turn right on a rather hidden

signposted footpath. On reaching the wide expanse of the next field turn left along its edge and keep to this direction, crossing further fields; emerge on a road and turn right. In 500m, now in **Porchfield** (pub), turn left on CB28, so starting a deviation from the official route using footpaths instead of roads. ▶

To reach the pub, continue a short way past the left turn.

Walk through one field and bear quarter-right through another to find and follow a hidden path in the trees, leading over a footbridge. Cross a lane to continue through another field. Almost at the end turn through a gap in the fence and, after exiting this new field, follow a signposted footpath left. Continue through two more fields and turn right at the lane beyond. At a T-junction turn left, now back on the official route. Soon cross Clamerkin Brook – the first of several crossings over Newtown Harbour tributaries – then at a junction in a further 500m turn right to continue towards **Newtown**.

After 550m turn left on a signposted footpath to walk through a series of very pretty meadows (National Trust), following yellow arrows, to emerge on a lane beside the former town pub, nicknamed Noah's Ark and defunct

Jetty, Newtown Harbour

since 1916. Descend past the 17th-century **Old Town Hall** (limited opening hours), and a bridge at the point where a brook feeds into Causeway Lake, to a T-junction.

Turn right and immediately locate and go through a gate hiding in the fence. Continue on the permissive path, ensuring you keep next to the road. When led back onto it, continue in your prevalent direction and in 200m branch right on a signposted track, swinging right with it after 250m. Beyond a footbridge over the Caul Bourne stream, the way becomes concrete. Continue to the main road in **Shalfleet** (pub, village shop) beside a welcome pub and bus stop. ◀

If you are flagging here, consider doing the remainder of the walk another day; not only is it remote, but its qualities should be savoured!

Turn right at the road and in 650m (on a descent) take the signposted footpath on the right, hiding in a hedge. You're now gradually making your way back to the coast. Just 60m after crossing Ningwood Lake in an idyllic setting, branch right on a minor path to keep near

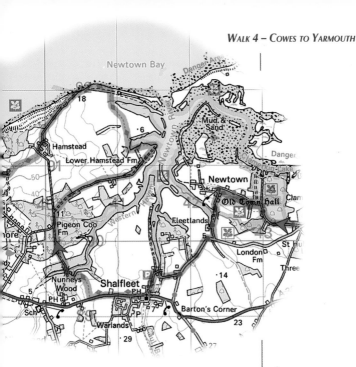

the water's edge, passing the most perfect picnic spot. Shortly rejoin the main path and turn right on the track ahead. In 700m, on an ascent, turn right on a new track. Pass **Lower Hamstead Farm** in 1.2km, and in a further 230m turn left on a signposted footpath – but not before a short detour ahead to admire one of the best views of Newtown Harbour.

Cross a series of boardwalks around one of the harbour inlets, then continue along the edge of a vast field. In 200m bear left over a stile into a parallel field and take the faint path half-right. And so, after a long absence, you return abruptly to the shoreline and turn left along the stony beach. Shortly forsake the beach for grass, and in 350m from the start of this shoreline section peek through a gap in the hedge to notice a memorial (Celtic cross) to two young brothers and a third man who drowned near here in the 1930s.

Shortly the path heads gradually back inland. Reach **Hamstead Farm** 1km from the memorial, and in a further 200m, just after the track swings left, go right on a sign-posted footpath. Cross a stile and walk round the left side of a field. Cross into the next field and a third field, turning left with the path. Shortly swing right to follow the CP sign, and cross a driveway after 200m to continue. Go left at the T-junction ahead and ignore ways off until, in 250m, the route turns right up West Close. In 150m turn left on a signposted footpath among scattered houses, still in a very remote and beautiful location. You soon enter Bouldnor Forest.

The mixed woodland (Corsican pine is dominant) and red-squirrel haven of **Bouldnor Forest** is under some threat due to coastal erosion eating away at Bouldnor Cliffs (the forest's front line of defence). The cliffs themselves are immensely fossil-rich. In Victorian times there were plans to inhabit the area, including constructing a pier – which was begun and can be seen at low tide – but the unfavourable terrain proved too much of an impediment.

View of Bouldnor Forest

In 200m ignore a broad left fork to continue in your current direction. Keep to the main path. In 1.2km you return (again rather abruptly) to the shoreline. Following signs, continue through more woodland back to the Newport–Yarmouth road (A3054) (700m) and mainstream civilisation once again. Turn right along the grass verge. Shortly beyond bus stops is a car park/viewpoint; at its start find and descend a slope to return to the shore. Follow the seawall as far as possible, ascend Yarmouth Common and turn right into the high street of **Yarmouth** (limited accommodation, pubs, cafés, restaurants, shops, toilets).

The sea wall near Yarmouth

> This delightful **high street** is sprinkled with distinguished 18th- and 19th-century houses and, nearer the town centre, independent shops and restaurants. Its charm is humbler and somehow more genuine than that of, for instance, the centre of Godshill.

At the T-junction in the town centre, go through the passageway opposite and turn left then right to reach the bus station.

WALK 5

Yarmouth to Alum Bay

Start	Yarmouth bus station/car park
Finish	Needles Park, Alum Bay
Distance	9.1km (5.7 miles)
Grade	Moderate (easy as far as Totland)
Time	3hrs
Refreshments	Colwell Bay (5km), Totland Pier (6.1km)
Public transport	*To start* Bus route 7. **Tip** In season, bus route 21 runs early morning from Newport to Yarmouth via Calbourne. The buses are open-top and hugely enjoyable in fine weather. The service is under-publicised and under-used. *From finish* Bus route 7, seasonal Needles Breezer.
Parking	Long-stay car park just east of the bus station (on bend)
Early finish	Colwell (4.4km, bus route 7 and Needles Breezer). At and beyond Totland Pier there are frequent opportunities to shorten the walk – head inland to eventually meet a B-road (bus route 7 and Needles Breezer).

A wonderful stage of the Coastal Path – beauty and interest from start to finish. From the understated port of Yarmouth, the route follows a sea wall to enter a lovely stretch of woodland in Fort Victoria Country Park. After a commanding view of Hurst Castle on the mainland, pleasant paths head briefly inland and return to the sea at pretty Colwell Bay (with sandy beach). Follow the shoreline to Totland Bay – stony but just as suitable for swimming as Colwell and with a pier that at the time of writing is being restored. There then follows a steep climb to the top of Headon Warren and a magnificent vista across to High Down, the Needles, and the Needles Park above Alum Bay – the final destination of both the north coast and south coast routes of the Coastal Path.

From the bus station in **Yarmouth** (limited accommodation, pubs, cafés, restaurants, shops, toilets), head west to cross the swing bridge over the Western Yar. Where

Map continues on
page 67

the road heads
inland turn right
on a signposted foot-
path, shortly walking
beside the sea. Just before the
sea wall ends, bear half-left on a broad woodland track
and turn right on the road above. In 80m bear left again
up a car-wide track, now in the mixed woodland of **Fort
Victoria Country Park**.

> **Fort Victoria** was one of many Palmerston Forts
> built around the island to repel any French inva-
> sion, and was considered especially useful given
> the narrowness of the Solent here. The remains of
> the fort have been converted into an aquarium,
> planetarium, model railway and marine heritage
> centre. Detour along the road for 200m to reach it.

Keep to the main path. Eventually climb steps, at the
top of which is a wonderful view towards Hurst Castle,
the closest point on the mainland to the island (just 0.8
miles).

The view to Hurst Castle

Hurst Castle served as the mainland's equivalent to Fort Victoria and Fort Albert (see below), but was built 300 years earlier at about the same time as Yarmouth Castle. It hosted King Charles I on his final, fateful journey from Carisbrooke to London, as well as other 17th-century prisoners.

Soon there is another incredible view towards Colwell Bay, Totland Bay (beyond), the Tennyson Monument on top of Tennyson Down, and the Needles. At the approach road to a holiday park turn left, then right at a junction (450m) to walk through another holiday park. Turn left at a T-junction and continue on a path between bushes to a junction (150m). ◄

Except at the highest tide walkers can take a worthwhile shortcut by turning right to the shore and walking along the beach to the huts on Colwell Bay.

Bear left at the junction and on reaching a road in **Colwell** turn right, shortly passing bus stops. Turn right onto Madeira Lane (200m), and just after the track swings right (350m) turn left on a path beside a metal pole. At the end, with a view towards Fort Albert and the mainland's Hurst Castle, turn left along the sea wall. The former was a 'partner' defence structure to Fort Victoria, but is now privately owned. Pass the huts at **Colwell Bay** mentioned earlier to continue along the wall to and beyond **Totland Pier** (a very lovely stretch).

Continue until you reach a brick hut, and climb the adjacent steps. Turn right on reaching a road, and after 300m bear right on a signposted footpath. Emerging in the open after 350m, ignore a right fork to ascend **Headon Warren**. On reaching an information board (150m) swing right with the

Sea wall, Totland Bay

On top of Headon Warren

clear path, and after 300m ignore a significant right fork. At the top of the hill turn right along the ridge, ignoring ways off, now with a spectacular panoramic view.

After 200m turn left off the ridge following the sign. Bear left after 250m in the direction of Alum Bay and left again at a path T-junction shortly after. Soon reach a driveway and turn left, ignoring the footpath immediately on the right. At the junction ahead turn right to reach the bus stop beside the entrance to the **Needles Park** above Alum Bay (bar, cafés, restaurant, shops, toilets). You might want to descend to the bay itself by chair lift (seasonal) or footpath.

SOUTH COAST

WALK 6
Sandown to Ventnor

Start	Sandown Pier
Finish	Ventnor
Distance	9.2km (5.8 miles)
Grade	Easy to Shanklin, then moderate
Time	3½hrs
Refreshments	A sprinkling of seasonal cafés between Sandown and Shanklin. One seasonal café beyond Shanklin.
Public transport	*To start* Bus routes 2, 3 and 8, and train (short walk); *from finish* Bus routes 3 and 6
Parking	Long-stay car park in Station Avenue; also possible beside the pier
Early finish	Lake station (1.2km), Shanklin Old Village (4.4km, bus route 3), top of Devil's Chimney (7.1km, bus route 3)

The heavily used cliff-top path between arguably the two premier resorts on the island, Sandown and Shanklin, makes for an easy, brisk hour's stroll and can even be enjoyed at night. After descending to the beach past the entrance to Shanklin Chine, the route climbs the numerous Appley steps to lovely Rylstone Gardens in the Old Village and continues up Luccombe Road with its fine, dignified houses. The Landslip follows – a riot of greenery with intermittent sea views. Make a short detour to the old church at Bonchurch, and end this particularly varied walk along the sea wall linking Bonchurch and Ventnor.

Facing the pier at **Sandown** (accommodation, supermarkets, pubs, cafés, restaurants, shops, toilets) turn right. After 150m go right by the Ferncliff Path sign to head steeply uphill. Shortly go left up steps and left at the top through Ferncliff Gardens to emerge on a cliff-top path

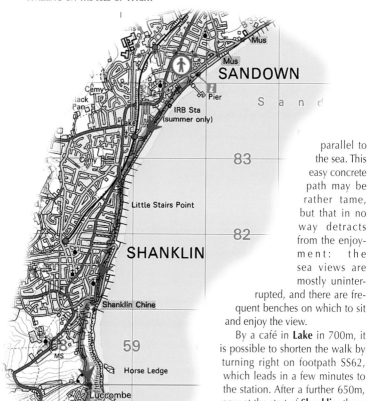

parallel to the sea. This easy concrete path may be rather tame, but that in no way detracts from the enjoyment: the sea views are mostly uninterrupted, and there are frequent benches on which to sit and enjoy the view.

By a café in **Lake** in 700m, it is possible to shorten the walk by turning right on footpath SS62, which leads in a few minutes to the station. After a further 650m, now at the start of **Shanklin**, those who would rather walk along the seafront can bear left down to the shore (SS65), but the recommended route is to continue ahead. Pass the seasonal lift (built 1891) in a further 1.1km and continue on the undulating path, soon passing the back gardens of some rather quaint-looking hotels in Keats Green, named after the poet, who frequently visited Shanklin. At the end of the green, descend past a metal barrier all the way to the shore, perhaps visiting **Shanklin Chine** halfway

Map continues on
page 73

Keats Green

down – it's worth paying the admission charge if only to experience the island's oldest tourist attraction.

> Beautifully foliaged **Shanklin Chine** was opened to the public as early as 1817, and was as popular in the Victorian era as it is now. As well as its pretty trails and diverse bird- and animal-life – including resident chipmunks – the Chine boasts a 12m (40ft) waterfall and romantic summer-night illuminations. There is also a permanent exhibition about the wartime Pipe Line Under The Ocean (PLUTO), which ran from the Chine to Cherbourg transporting petrol for Allied troops. The idea came from Lord Mountbatten and was apparently very successful – the enemy never knew about it, and 56,000 gallons of petrol per day was transported this way during 1944.

Turn sharp right at the bottom of the slope to walk along the shore; pass the Fisherman's Cottage, then after 150m go sharp right up the inconspicuous 'Appley Steps'. At the top, although the Coastal Path continues straight ahead, why not detour through pretty Rylstone Gardens

71

To end the walk, or perhaps have lunch, turn sharp right on exiting the gardens to reach the centre of Shanklin Old Village (pubs, cafés, restaurants, shops, toilets) via the upper gate of the Chine. Bus stops are just up the hill.

first? Continue with the sea to the right this time, then when the path ends at a viewpoint return through the park, pausing to admire the charming small hotel – once a gentlemen's club – in its grounds and perhaps having a cuppa in one of the tea rooms.

Aim for the far right corner of the park, with a view down to Shanklin Chine; pass an aviary, bear left, and then bear right at a sculpture. Exiting the gardens, turn right then immediately left to ascend Luccombe Road with its large elegant houses. ◄ In 400m turn right on a signposted footpath into a field and immediately left, keeping close to the hedge (or stay on the road if too muddy). Go over a stile in the far corner to return to and continue along the road, enjoying lovely sea views.

Keep straight ahead at a junction and shortly continue on a footpath through woodland. Ignore ways off. Enter the **Landslip** (so called because of the erosion and intermittent landslides that have affected the area since the last ice age) after 1.1km (up steps), again ignoring ways off the main path and following Coastal Path signs.

Sweep of Sandown Bay from Luccombe

After 450m, to shorten the walk, take V65c up the notorious 'Devil's Chimney': a tough 10mins climb up 225 steps, one section narrowly wedged between cliffs. ▶ Otherwise, the path continues to wind around the Landslip's foliage. After 650m, turn right – initially up three steps. After 150m bear left and left again at the next junction, but not before detouring a short way to the right to see isolated St Boniface Church at **Bonchurch**, nestled in its delightful churchyard.

At the road behind the Smugglers Haven turn right for bus stops.

Shortly after this junction there is a choice of paths; take either, as both eventually emerge on a sea wall at Wheelers Bay (if taking the upper path bear left at the end). Continue along it to reach the seafront at **Ventnor** (accommodation, supermarket, pubs, cafés, restaurants, shops, toilets). For the high street and bus stop, turn sharp right up the slope opposite the Hygeia mosaic at the start of the front, and continue up Pier Street to the T-junction. Poke your nose into Alexandra Gardens on the way: Elgar honeymooned at number three.

73

WALK 7
Ventnor to Chale

Start	Ventnor seafront
Finish	Chale
Distance	10km (6.3 miles)
Grade	Moderate
Time	4hrs
Refreshments	Steephill Cove (1.7km), Ventnor Botanic Garden (2km), St Lawrence (4.2km), Blackgang Chine (9.4km)
Public transport	*To start* Bus routes 3 and 6; *from finish* Bus route 6
Parking	Eastern Esplanade or La Falaise long-stay car parks
Early finish	St Lawrence (4km, bus route 6). Additionally, between Niton and Chale the route is never far from the road (bus route 6).

This must count among the best walks on the island, so pick a sunny day to appreciate it fully. After ascending the cliffs west of Ventnor and passing the botanic gardens, the walk reaches the classy village of St Lawrence, a peaceful and – so it would seem – eminently desirable place to live. Ascend onto even higher cliffs and soon there are magnificent views towards St Catherine's Lighthouse and a quite special sense of serenity, even on this most serene of islands. But the best is yet to come as Windy Corner is approached and the entire southwest coast (Back of the Wight) is spread out before you, all the way to the iconic white cliffs of High Down. The route descends first to the country's oldest amusement park at Blackgang Chine and, finally, to Chale – perhaps visit the church (or the pub!) while waiting for the bus.

Lizards were introduced to Ventnor in the early 19th century and a colony has developed on the cliffs around this car park – so keep a look out!

Walk west along the esplanade at **Ventnor** (accommodation, supermarket, pubs, cafés, restaurants, shops, toilets) and continue uphill. Keep left beyond La Falaise car park to find and follow a sea-hugging cliff path: coastal walking doesn't get much better than this! ◀

Stay on the paths nearest the sea, eventually reaching Steephill Cove (restaurants/cafés, toilets), a lovely low-key place to rest and perhaps swim. Ascend the slope at the far end of the cove, turning sharp left after 40m, ascending steps and turning left again. The path soon merges with the seaward side of **Ventnor Botanic Garden**. You may wish to take time to explore the garden: there is a café with a pleasant outdoor seating area.

> **Ventnor Botanic Garden** is protected from northerly winds by its Undercliff setting, and its warm and sunny microclimate has enabled unusual exotic and subtropical species to thrive here – even cacti are grown, although the excellent website (**www.botanic.co.uk**) admits this is a somewhat experimental project! There is a Mediterranean garden, complete with an olive grove and lizards; a palm garden featuring the oldest palms in Britain; and Australian, New Zealand, Oriental and South African gardens among others. There is also an interesting display about the days when the garden was part of the Royal National Hospital for Diseases of the Chest, founded in 1868.

The path soon comes out into the open; from this point fewer walkers are likely to be encountered. The path stays on top of the sea cliffs for about another 1.25km, then turns inland, now in **St Lawrence** (village shop). In 150m turn left through a gate; then where the main path swings left, branch right, ignoring path offshoots, and turn left at the lane above. Turn right at the T-junction and walk up to the main road, beside bus

Map continues on page 77

75

stops. Continue up Spindlers Road, past the turn for the village shop. At Seven Sisters Road ahead turn left. (Alternatively, go right for a pleasant 20min-return detour to the old church and peace gardens; descend right at The Shute.) In 80m take footpath V81 which ascends steeply to 'High Hat': the views from up here, towering over St Lawrence, eclipse even the earlier ones.

Continue west along the cliff path. ◀ Swing left at a path junction in a further 800m (shortly after the path turns inland). At the road turn right and immediately sharp left up a driveway, soon with incredible views of **St Catherine's Point** – the island's southern tip – and its tenant lighthouse.

Pass a two-armed signpost and bench 700m from the road. To descend to the lighthouse from here see Walk 24, but otherwise continue – now on the west of the island and about to start your exploration of the south-west coast. The famous chalk cliffs of High Down soon come into view, and eventually – just short of what is known as Windy Corner – there is the first view of the entire southwest coastline (Back of the Wight): one of the island's iconic vistas!

The path shortly swings inland, the view now encompassing Blackgang Chine below (ignore a steeply descending path towards it), and emerges at a car park; near the

After 1.7km take the footpath to Niton if you need refreshments or wish to end the walk – you should reach the store and bus stops at Niton within 30mins.

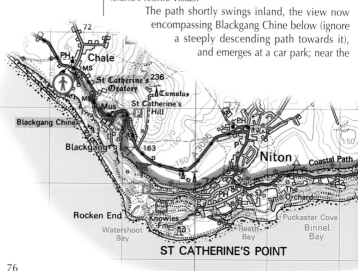

road turn left through a wooden gate on a descending path. In 200m maintain your current direction along the right edge of a field. Turn right over a stile after 80m and continue along the roadside verge, bearing right at the **Blackgang** roundabout (or left for the short detour to **Blackgang Chine** and its adjacent café).

View towards St Catherine's Lighthouse

Although, because of frequent landslips, the chine itself no longer exists, since 1843 **Blackgang Chine** has been the site of one of the island's main attractions, an understated but surprisingly enjoyable, old-fashioned amusement park enhanced by its cliff-top garden setting. One of its first exhibits, still on show today, was a whale skeleton found on the shore – apparently during a visit by Queen Mary a bone knocked off

View towards Blackgang Chine and Back of the Wight

the Queen's hat, immediately after which it was cut off! Remarkably the park is still owned by the family who built it (the Dabells), although it has been a frequent victim of erosion, notably in 1994 when a sizeable chunk was destroyed.

After a further 300m turn left onto C15, then right at a T-junction. Back at the road turn left and immediately right past the church at **Chale** (limited accommodation, pub) to the bus stops.

Chale Church retains few of its 12th-century origins, having been largely reconstructed in the 15th century, when the tower was added. The village is dripping with tales of smugglers and shipwrecks, and the churchyard is full of unfortunates who perished at sea.

WALK 8

Chale to Brook

Start	Chale Church
Finish	Brook Chine
Distance	12.7km (7.9 miles)
Grade	Easy apart from short steep descents and ascents at Shepherd's and Marsh Chines
Time	4hrs
Refreshments	Café at Isle of Wight Pearl (9.5km)
Public transport	*To start* Bus route 6; *from finish* Bus route 12 (limited service)
Parking	Car park about 200m north of the church
Early finish	Near Brighstone (8km) or anywhere along the coastal road for the afternoon Island Coaster bus service

The Back of the Wight's heavily eroded coastline is bleak, wild and ruggedly beautiful. Dubbed 'The Ships' Graveyard', it has claimed countless vessels and lives over the centuries, with many of the victims ending up in Chale churchyard. Contrast this stretch of the Coastal Path with that from Cowes to Gurnard – both offer very different ways of experiencing the island's coastline. That said, in the right conditions this should be an easy, serene walk with lovely views, perfect for contemplation or conversation. But pick a calm day: in rain or even just brisk northerly or westerly winds the outing can turn into a slog, especially as there is little shelter en route and often a long way to a bus stop.

Chale (limited accommodation, pub) is a small, indistinct village, so those coming by bus need to be eagle-eyed or ask the driver for Chale Church. At the T-junction by the church turn right.

> This is **Military Road**, constructed in the 1930s to replace a 19th-century defence track. It follows the coastline from Chale to Freshwater Bay, and because of this is under constant threat of erosion.

79

Opposite the pub driveway turn left on footpath C17 sea-bound, following New Chine. Soon the path swings right along the cliff-top, with the entire southwest coastline spread out ahead. About 1.1km after leaving the road, follow C18 back to it and turn left.

> The diversion is due to **Whale Chine** a short distance ahead – 43m (140ft) deep and unusually bare of vegetation, it is by far the most impressive of the chines encountered on this walk, but not possible to cross. There is dispute over the origin of its name – a corruption of 'Wavell', perhaps, the name of the 16th- and 17th-century owners of nearby Atherfield Farm, or in memory of an 18th-century beached whale.

A path may be open leading down the chine onto the beach – for very fit people only!

Whale Chine

At the far end of a car park return to the cliff, now on the other side of the chine. ◄ Some 2.5km later is **Shepherd's Chine**, less dramatic than Whale Chine and navigable. Walk inland to find the descending path; turn left at the bottom beside the remains of a reservoir and pump house, and climb the steep slope at the end (or detour down steps for the beach).

Shep▮

View towards Atherfield Point

Map continues on page 83

45

Ashhill Fm

Little Atherfield

37

42

Atherfield Green

Atherfield Fm

83

Pyle

...ld Point

39

Westside Fm.

Whale Chine

Walpan

56

72

PH

Chale

MS

St Catherine's Oratory

236

Chale Bay

MS

Mus

St Cathe

Blackgang Chine

Blackgang

81

If you require some lunch, have had enough, or bus times are tight, after 1.4km go over two stiles in succession and continue up to Brighstone (under 30mins walk away).

Effects of erosion

Walk around the next chine (Cowleaze) and about 1km later swing right on a rise, with the village of Brighstone now visible. Descend and bear left to keep walking along the cliff. ◀ Soon descend and reascend **Grange Chine** to continue along the cliff-top. Reach the incongruous Isle of Wight Pearl after 850m: it is said to house the largest collection of pearl jewellery in the UK, but walkers may be more attracted to the very welcome café, the only place for refreshments and shelter directly en route.

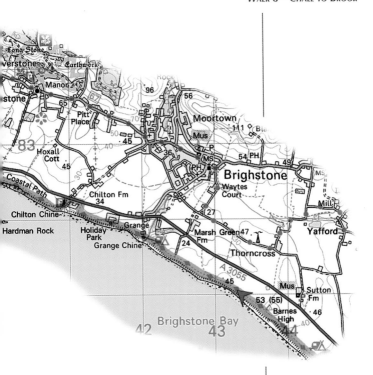

Make your way to the road behind the complex, turn left to cross over **Chilton Chine**, and return to the sea. Some 2.5km later, the path approaches the cottages at Brook Chine. Bear right towards the cottages on a grassy path to find and follow a track leading to the road and bus stops at **Brook** (limited accommodation, pub at nearby Hulverstone). Alternatively, to continue along the Coastal Path bear sharp left on a grassy path just before the road.

WALK 9

Brook to Alum Bay

Start	Brook Chine
Finish	Needles Park, Alum Bay
Distance	10.3km (6.5 miles)
Grade	Moderate
Time	4hrs
Refreshments	Freshwater Bay (4.2km), tearoom at Needles Old Battery (admission fee – 9km)
Public transport	*To start* Bus route 12; *from finish* Bus route 7
Parking	Car park at Brook Chine
Early finish	There are several opportunities before Freshwater Bay to return to the coastal road (bus route 12); otherwise, the seasonal Needles Breezer at the Needles Batteries (9km)

If you are on the island for only a short time then, good weather permitting, this is one of the walks you shouldn't miss. Unlike the official Coastal Path, which curiously stops short on High Down before turning round to Alum Bay, this alternative carries on to the National Trust's Old and New Batteries (Victorian defence installations) and remarkable viewpoints towards the famous Needles and Scratchell's Bay. First there is the cliff-top walk above Compton Bay with the chalk cliffs of High Down drawing ever closer – look out for surfers and kitesurfers. Then, after Freshwater Bay, comes the ascent to the Tennyson Monument and the thrilling approach to 'the end of the island', a narrow peninsula with the sea on both sides. There is more cliff-top walking after the about-turn and before the short final descent to the Needles Park on top of the cliffs of Alum Bay.

From the road junction at Brook Chine (pub at nearby Hulverstone), follow footpath BS79 parallel to the chine and turn left at the car park to find the onward path. Note the contrast between the clay cliffs now underfoot and the chalk cliffs of Tennyson Down and West High

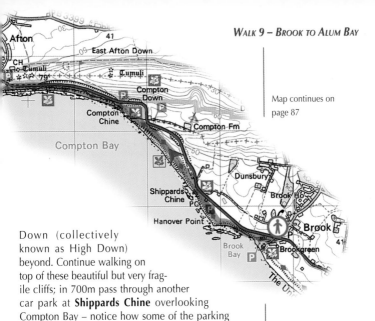

Map continues on page 87

Down (collectively known as High Down) beyond. Continue walking on top of these beautiful but very fragile cliffs; in 700m pass through another car park at **Shippards Chine** overlooking Compton Bay – notice how some of the parking spaces have been lost to erosion! ▶

After a further 1.1km go over a stile and turn left before the gates ahead to continue on top of the cliff. Soon skirt around narrow Compton Chine and ascend to the coastal road. Walk along the verge initially, and at the brow of the hill take the parallel path, soon descending seaward. On reaching a Victorian memorial to a dead child, bear left to continue towards **Freshwater Bay** (pub, café, shop, toilets); just before the final descent, bear left down steps to approach via its sea wall. At the bus stops on the other side of the bay turn left, and in 50m turn right to ascend Tennyson Down – although you may wish to detour to Fort Redoubt ahead.

> **Fort Redoubt** is one of the island's many mid-Victorian Palmerston Forts, built to repel a possible French invasion. It is now a private residence, but some of the original features can still be seen.

Compton Bay is the best place on the 'Dinosaur Island' to spot dinosaur fossils (at low tide). There are steps from the car park to the shore.

85

This is where the drama really starts: the north coast is soon visible as well as a wonderful view back towards Freshwater Bay and the entire Back of the Wight, and there is a sense of how wild and narrow the peninsula is becoming. Approaching the **Tennyson Monument** look back for a new view over Freshwater. The monument is about 1.7km from Freshwater Bay – a good place to take stock and linger a while.

West High Down – the western tip of the island

The **Tennyson Monument**, with its granite cross, was erected in 1897 at the highest point of High Down in memory of the famous Poet Laureate who frequently left his Freshwater home (Farringford) to walk on this down, where the air, so he said, is 'worth sixpence a pint'. 'The Charge of the Light Brigade' is one work which was written on the down.

The Needles

Strike out towards West High Down, always keeping to the centre of the ridge – over to the right is Headon Warren, which is explored in Walk 5, and in clear conditions Bournemouth and the Isle of Purbeck are visible. Eventually the route follows the northern coastline as much as the southern! Approaching a fence (2.2km from the monument) bear left through a gate. Skirt to the left of the transmitter and descend to a drive; follow the sign opposite to the viewpoint – well worth the short detour for the view of **Scratchell's Bay** and **the Needles**.

> **The Needles** are three separate rock towers off the island's westernmost point, and the most famous, distinctive and dramatic location on the island. There were originally four 'needles', and it is ironic that the only apparently needle-like rock of the four, known as 'Lot's Wife', was the one to collapse (in 1764). At one time the Needles were part of a chalk ridge that extended to Handfast Point near Swanage on the mainland, but the ridge had been all but eroded by 3000BC. The lighthouse on the furthest rock started functioning on New Year's Day 1859 and has a 22.5km (14 mile) range. Since 1994 it has been – like all functioning British lighthouses today – very unromantically controlled by the General Lighthouse Authority in Harwich.

Return to the drive and turn left to walk towards the New Battery.

The **New Battery** was completed in 1895 as a replacement for the decaying Old Battery on the cliff below. Despite having some limited role in both World Wars, it really came into its own between 1956 and 1971 as a site for testing firstly intercontinental ballistic missiles and then space rocket engines. There is an exhibition with limited opening hours.

On reaching the Needles Breezer bus stop (50m) descend the adjacent concrete walkway towards the Old Battery – but eschew the penultimate flight of steps for a stony path and look down from the corner: below mighty cliffs, and accessible only by sea, Scratchell's Bay is one of the most dramatic sights of the walk. ◄ Continue up the drive by the **Old Battery** entrance, the multi-shaded cliffs of Alum Bay now ahead.

In season, frequent boat trips operate from Alum Bay to Scratchell's Bay via the Needles.

The **Old Battery**, completed in 1863, was originally a Palmerston Fort, like Fort Redoubt. It saw action in both World Wars, notably the Second, when its guns were successful in destroying enemy torpedo boats and planes. The battery can be visited in season.

At the junction ahead turn left up steps to continue on a ledge. Pass concrete steps on the right after 200m. For the most dramatic approach to Alum Bay, drop down the grass (very steeply) 30m beyond these steps, on a path of sorts, to walk closer to the cliff edge. The path should not be dangerous, although care is needed due to potential erosion and possible strong winds. Once back on the drive, swing left to follow it down to the Needles Park at **Alum Bay** (bar, cafés, restaurant, shops, toilets). The bus stop is by the park entrance.

WEST WIGHT

Freshwater Bay and Back of the Wight (Walk 15)

WALK 10

Shorwell circular

Start/Finish	Crown Inn, Shorwell
Distance	14km (8.8 miles)
Grade	Moderate
Time	5hrs
Refreshments	None en route
Public transport	Bus route 12 (limited service). A car is ideal transport as buses run only every 2 or 3 hours, but if you have long to wait in Shorwell you could always repair to the pub.
Parking	Crown Inn car park (customers only).
Early finish	Newport–Shorwell road (B3323) (6.4km and 8km, bus route 12)

The downland to the immediate northwest and northeast of Shorwell is off the beaten track even for walkers, yet is surprisingly appealing and makes for a wonderful outing if the weather stays good. The first stage leads up onto Limerstone Down, but then instead of going through Brighstone Forest the walk heads onto the plateau of Cheverton Down, descends to a very remote valley and meanders through the deciduous woodland of Rowborough Bottom. Back on the Newport to Shorwell road the walk continues with an ascent of Chillerton Down and draws closer towards its mighty transmitter, a significant landmark that can be seen across the island. The approach back to Shorwell is delightful, and highlights the extent of the woodland immediately surrounding the village.

Facing the Crown Inn at **Shorwell** (limited accommodation, pub, shop) turn left and in 150m abruptly right on bridleway SW6 opposite a very elegant detached house. Beyond the gate ahead ascend half-left through the pathless field. Soon, spot and cross a metal gate in the far corner to continue on a grassy path – look back to see Shorwell behind you.

In 150m bear right onto a ledge, parallel to Limerstone Down to the north (which will be ascended shortly). Continue through a gate and ignore ways off the ridge, eventually skirting above two sides of a vast field and ascending to the fieldgate in the distance. Keep ignoring ways off this final stage of ascent, but look down to observe the convoluted topography of the low hills around Brighstone.

On the ridge near the top of **Limerstone Down** turn right. Make a short detour to the toposcope at the top where, naturally, the best view yet awaits. Then continue on the previous path until you are level with barns away to the left (260m). Here turn left through a fieldgate (there may be a white arrow on the fencepost) and continue anticlockwise around the field perimeter. With the route heading towards Brighstone Forest, continue in the same direction when the fence swings right, and turn right into a smaller field after 70m. Keep to its right edge, continue through a further field, and turn right on exiting.

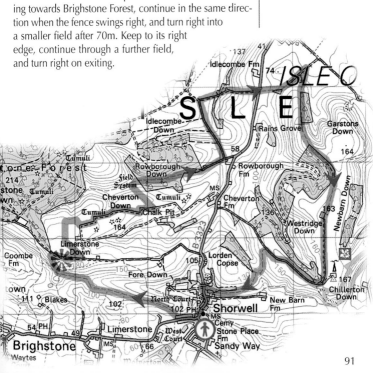

Brighstone Forest from Cheverton Down

At a junction, turn left along a wide stony track – now on **Cheverton Down** and facing Chillerton Down across the valley which will be climbed later. In 1km turn left down an equally broad track. Ignore a left fork after 150m to continue the descent, now on a grassy path, to the bottom of the remote valley. Turn right, shortly entering the woodland of Rowborough Bottom. Stay on the main track through the wood – a beautiful stroll.

In 1km – or about 100m before the Newport–Shorwell road (B3323) – either turn left on a wide grassy path which soon merges with a track and ascends steeply; or, to end the walk, continue to the road and turn right for bus stops. When the main track eventually swings left, turn right through a gate to descend back to the road, which marks the end of the longest and most strenuous half of the walk. Bus stops are to the north, but the onward route takes N137a, almost opposite.

Turn right at a track T-junction in 550m – at the foot of an incline with a view towards Carisbrooke Castle and Church – and branch right into woodland in a further 90m (N146). The path shortly leaves the wood to ascend **Chillerton Down**. On reaching the top, continue between rows of conifers, and keep walking towards the slender and quite awe-inspiring 230m (755ft) transmitter.

> It could be argued that the **transmitter** complements – rather than detracts from – the stark beauty of the landscape. The most visually prominent landmark on the island, it was built in 1958, used for television until 1985, and currently broadcasts local FM and DAB radio.

Eventually the trees are left behind and vistas open up west and east, all under magnificent skies. Truly a special place, and chances are you will have it all to yourself. Pass a pair of isolated barns – somewhere to shelter if caught up here in a storm – and plough on towards the transmitter. At the T-junction just beyond it, go right, the Back of the Wight coastline now visible again.

In 800m, look out for and turn left on a broad stony track. Just past a cattle grid with **New Barn Farm** opposite bear right, and near the top of the short ascent branch left on a faint grassy path (the higher of the two possible

Rowborough Bottom

options), soon with lovely belts of trees on both sides. Approach **Shorwell** above its thatched cottages (all very picturesque), but instead of descending towards it at the end of the field bear right to find a path leading through a wood and across the evocative wooden footbridge over Shorwell Shute, which those travelling from Newport would have spotted earlier.

Once over the bridge turn left, and left again on the drive below – although do detour right briefly to see the entrance to Jacobean **North Court**, one of the village's three manor houses (West Court and Wolverton Manor, both slightly older, are the other two). Back on the road, turn right to continue past the village shop and church to arrive back at the Crown Inn.

WALK 11

Shorwell to Niton

Start	Crown Inn, Shorwell
Finish	Niton
Distance	12.4km (7.7 miles)
Grade	Fairly easy to Chale, then moderate
Time	4hrs
Refreshments	None en route
Public transport	*To start* Bus route 12; *from finish* Bus route 6
Parking	Crown Inn car park (customers only)
Early finish	Near Chale (7.1km, bus route 6)

This walk links two of the principal villages on the south of the island and can be said to have two parts. The first is low key and remote but still lovely and varied, meandering through empty, atmospheric fields and woods near to, but just out of sight of, the sea. After crossing the Newport–Chale road, the second part of the route ascends St Catherine's Down and visits both the Hoy Monument and St Catherine's Oratory Lighthouse, the latter with stupendous views. Pick a sunny day for this one!

From the Crown Inn at **Shorwell** (limited accommodation, pub, shop) walk west along the road and in 200m turn left on footpath SW3. Cross a stile (150m) and turn right along the field edge. Near the end of the field, turn left to cross another stile and continue over wooden planks through a wood. At a path junction turn right, then almost immediately left over a footbridge to continue on concrete.

> This is the estate of **Wolverton Manor**. The manor house, on the left, is a late Tudor property with 18th-century additions that is still a private residence.

Maintain your current direction at a lane, and at the next junction turn left and right shortly after (SW20). After a short, sharp ascent, a thoughtfully placed bench provides a welcome place to rest and gaze at the view ahead – it doesn't get any more tranquil than this! Continue on the pathless grass and, just after crossing a hedgerow, descend sharp right on a very faint path. You will soon be climbing St Catherine's Down, visible in the left distance.

Wolverton Manor

Cross a track and continue in the same direction through the field opposite. When a hedgerow bars the way, turn left then shortly right through a gate. At a junction with a concrete track (750m) turn right, then after 200m take SW21 through the centre of the field. Keep to the right-hand side of the next field, then in 200m turn right over two stiles and continue towards the hillock ahead. Curve round the hillock with the field track and continue through the next field, keeping close to the left-hand side.

At the field end, turn right to locate the entrance to the next field. Cross a stream (200m) and turn left. After 400m keep straight ahead with a rise on the left, angling towards then following the fence on the right. Ignore ways off, then just before an isolated house turn right (C28). Ignore ways off to walk through a lovely stretch of woodland

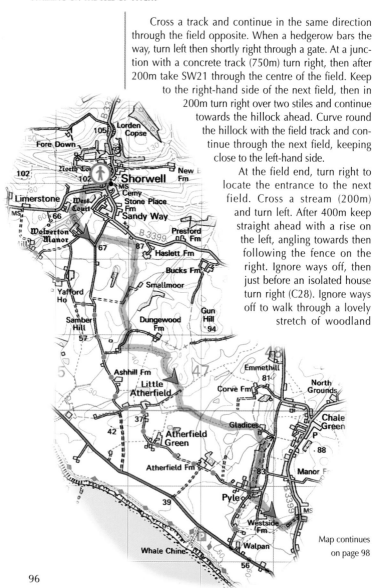

Map continues
on page 98

Pyle Manor

and past late 17th-century **Pyle Manor**. At a road junction continue on Southdown, then almost immediately turn left on C23 steeply uphill, turning left at the top, now with a clear view of both the Hoy Monument (left) and St Catherine's Oratory ('Pepper Pot') (right) on St Catherine's Down ahead.

On reaching a lane turn right then shortly left (C20). In 150m bear left, cross a stream (200m), then immediately turn left. On reaching a building on the left, bear half-right to reach the Newport–Chale road (B3399). ▶

Cross the road to take C4. Keep near the right edge of two successive fields and the left edge of the next three. Bear left round a hillock, then very shortly look for and climb a steep grassy embankment on the left. Cross a stile to continue along the bottom of the escarpment, now with a great 180° view including Chale and the coastline behind you. In 250m cross a stile on the right; then at a path junction after 350m, turn right along a signposted bridleway. After 250m go sharp right on C6 to ascend to the **Hoy Monument**.

If you don't feel like tackling St Catherine's Down, bus stops are about 50m on the right.

The 22m (72ft) **Hoy Monument**, named after the purchaser rather than the dedicatee, was erected by trader Michael Hoy to commemorate a visit to England by Tsar Alexander I in 1814, although ironically there is a plaque commemorating British losses (against Russian forces) in the Crimean War on the southern side. There is something rather lonely and melancholic about the monument's location, somewhat enclosed on three sides of a narrow ridge: quite the obverse to the spectacular vista from the nearby Pepper Pot.

Walk south along the grassy plateau, this time with a marvellous view east (the large village is Whitwell). In about 600m, beside a post with blue arrows, take either fork. On reaching a gate bear half-left

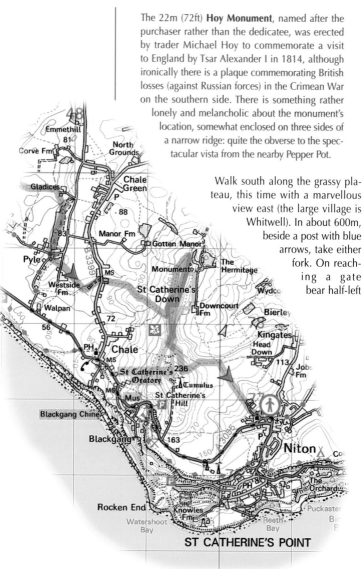

and turn right at a fence to ascend St Catherine's Hill and eventually reach the **Oratory Lighthouse**.

> **St Catherine's Oratory Lighthouse** (called the Pepper Pot for obvious reasons) has more visitors than the Hoy Monument to the north, being better known and more easily accessible. Situated on top of St Catherine's Hill – at 235m (771ft) one of the highest points on the island – it was completed in 1328 by a landowner who was ordered by church courts to build it as punishment for stealing (or receiving stolen) French wine. Solitary monks used to man the lighthouse until the adjoining oratory was demolished during the Dissolution of the Monasteries. An increasing number of shipwrecks led to work commencing on a new lighthouse close by in 1785, but only the foundation stones are visible (below the radio mast and nicknamed the Salt Pot), as it was never completed. Instead the decision was made to build the current gleaming St Catherine's Lighthouse on the southern tip of the island.

Opposite the entrance to the lighthouse is a white trig point; cross the stile beside it to continue across the field, with a sensational view. Notice your destination (Niton) down on the right. Go through a gate and bear half-left on a faint path, shortly skirting around a hollow on the right, and soon picking up a wide grassy path with a fence on the left. Go through a gate and continue on an enclosed path. Just past two gates and a stile (250m) turn right on a path which descends all the way to the Norman church at **Niton** (supermarket, pub, food shops, toilets).

WALK 12
Brighstone circular

Start/Finish	Three Bishops pub, Brighstone
Distance	11.4km (7.1 miles)
Grade	Moderate
Time	3½hrs
Refreshments	Mottistone Manor Garden (admission fee – 7.5km)
Public transport	Bus route 12 (limited service)
Parking	Warnes Lane car park (behind the Three Bishops pub)
Early finish	Mottistone (7.5km, bus route 12)

This is a walk of great contrasts, featuring open downland, deep forest, coast path, and a liberal scattering of wonderful views. The 3km middle section passes through Brighstone Forest, which has a certain majesty, and to walk through it can be quite a humbling experience. There are few sounds other than birdsong; route-finding is straightforward, and fellow walkers are few and far between – perfect for long conversation or solitary contemplation! The route descends to the Long Stone, arguably the most important prehistoric monument on the island, before arriving at Mottistone, with its lovely church and National Trust manor house and garden. The walk may be cut short here, but it would be a shame to miss the cliff-top stretch back to Brighstone.

From the Three Bishops pub at **Brighstone** (limited accommodation, pub, restaurant/café, food shops, toilets), walk towards the newsagents and turn right up North Street, one of the island's most unashamedly olde-worlde streets with its cute post office, National Trust shop and small museum. Cross the T-junction ahead to continue on bridleway BS81. In 340m, branch left off the ascending track to come out into the open. Branch right immediately to ascend steeply over grass. At the top of the steep incline bear left, still ascending, now with a wonderful vista of Brighstone and the sea.

View towards the Back of Wight coastline, with the Isle of Purbeck in the distance

At a crossroads of grassy paths go right, shortly descending beside the edge of a field. The majestic spectacle of Limerstone Down is ahead; soon you will be walking along its ridge. At the T-junction, take the lower of the two adjacent parallel paths. Stay on this enclosed path until another T-junction is reached and turn left to ascend **Limerstone Down**. A truly stunning view soon appears, encompassing the eastern coastline of the Isle of Purbeck on a clear day. At the top of the down, cross the track to continue within **Brighstone Forest**.

> The sprawling, predominantly broadleaved **Brighstone Forest** is the island's largest, although Parkhurst is a very close second. Planted only in the middle of the 20th century, it nevertheless has something of a mystical air about it, and walking through it is always a pleasure. There is frequent felling, but conservation work is underway to diversify the forest's (currently mainly beech) content and improve conditions for the red squirrel population.

Bear left after 200m, and at a crossroads (150m) turn left onto a broad track. Cross the Tennyson Trail and take the descending track opposite, deeper into the forest. Cross a road (1.2km) and continue on CB17. After a further 1.1km cross over a major path crossroads, and on finally emerging from the forest swing left on the grassy path. Immediately beyond a Tennyson Trail signpost and dual-coast view (40m), turn left on a hidden bridleway. Stay on the ridge – the view of forest, downs and sea is the finest so far and arguably one of the most aesthetically pleasing on the entire island.

In 600m cross a metal gate to continue your descent. At a T-junction turn left, shortly reaching the

See Walk 13.

prehistoric **Long Stone**. ◄ Walk around the Stone on the stony track, in 300m turning sharp right on a wide grassy path (about a 330° turn). Then on a left bend in a further 300m, turn left through a kissing gate onto a path that meanders through pretty woodland. Bear left at a junction in 200m, shortly arriving at the village of

Mottistone. The manor house and bus stops are to the left.

Mottistone Church

> The name **Mottistone** probably comes from the alternative name for the Long Stone ('Moot Stone'). The village's manor house was mentioned in the *Domesday book*, but the current house is Tudor in origin and was originally home to the Cheke family; one resident, Sir John Cheke, was tutor to King Edward VI. The house was restored in 1926 by a notable island family, the Seelys, or to be precise the first Baron Mottistone, and the family bequeathed the estate to the National Trust in 1963. It is still lived in by family members, and currently opened to the public for guided tours one day a year. The gardens, however, are open most days. Mottistone Church is 12th century in origin, with substantial 15th-century and Victorian additions and alterations.

To continue to Brighstone, take Church Lane near the bus stops and continue into Ridget Lane, which becomes a track leading down to the coastal road; cross the road to reach the sea and turn left on the Coastal Path. On reaching **Chilton Chine** turn inland and recross the coast road to continue on BS71. On reaching tarmac continue in your current direction, then just before a left bend take BS62 on the right. Cross Galley Lane (750m) and continue on BS24. Turn right on a residential road, then almost immediately left on BS25 back to the Three Bishops.

WALK 13

Brighstone to Yarmouth

Start	Three Bishops pub, Brighstone
Finish	Yarmouth
Distance	11.3km (7.1 miles)
Grade	Moderate
Time	3½hrs
Refreshments	None en route
Public transport	*To start* Bus route 12; *from finish* Bus route 7. **Tip** In season, bus route 21 runs twice in the late afternoon to Newport via Calbourne. The buses are open-top and hugely enjoyable in fine weather. The service is under-publicised and under-used.
Parking	Warnes Lane car park (behind the Three Bishops pub)
Early finish	Thorley (9.2km, bus route 7)

A pleasant meander through the surprisingly sizeable outskirts of Brighstone leads into Grammars Common – a beautiful, solitary hillside wood, which is likely to linger in the memory. The walk descends and reascends to the Long Stone – some 5000 years old – following which a balcony path provides stunning views of the Back of the Wight. After passing Grade II listed Shalcombe Manor, the walk takes on a different feel as it heads north through the rolling fields of lonely rural West Wight – delightful when covered in rapeseed in late spring. After a second beautiful wood, Mill Copse, the walk emerges at the Western Yar and travels beside it the short distance into Yarmouth.

From the Three Bishops pub in **Brighstone** (limited accommodation, pub, restaurant/café, food shops, toilets), walk towards the newsagents and turn right up North Street, one of the island's most unashamedly olde-worlde streets with its cute post office, National Trust shop and small museum. Turn left at the T-junction and in 300m left again (footpath BS38). Turn right at a lane and in 150m turn left (BS39). Reaching another road turn right and continue on the path at the end of the road. Turn left on a path between animal enclosures (just before the current path also swings left). Shortly after starting to follow a farm drive turn right (BS66) and ascend, soon with the ubiquitous but always delightful sea view, and Brighstone now below and behind you. Soon enter Grammars Common, a mainly coniferous wood idyllically situated. Bear left at the initial

Grammars Common

Map continues on page 107

The Long Stone

fork to continue to a path T-junction. Turn right to remain inside the wood, with a view now to High Down. Turn left at another T-junction to continue the ascent deeper into the wood. Eventually the way leads between gorse bushes and into a lovely grassy glade. At its end swing left and descend to a lane. Turn right, and then left after 70m (BS84) to continue up to the **Long Stone**.

The **Long Stone** is actually two stones of iron sandstone, the larger 4m (13ft) high, which formed the eastern end of a Neolithic burial mound – or long barrow – constructed some 5000 years ago. The form of the barrow can still be made out behind the stones. Its significance as a meeting place led to the Saxons calling it the 'Moot Stone', which, it is believed, led to the naming of the nearby village of Mottistone.

Turn right on the track, which soon becomes an exposed balcony path with one of the most comprehensive views of the Back of the Wight coastline (Blackgang to High Down). But all great things must pass, and eventually the path descends gradually to enter more woodland. After walking 900m from the Long Stone, just before a drive visible ahead (to Grade II listed **Brook Hill House**), turn right abruptly on a narrow footpath marked by a yellow arrow and emerge in a field.

Built by the Seely family in 1901, **Brook Hill House** was subsequently owned by JB Priestley, author of *An Inspector Calls*. The house is situated in a commanding hillside position (there are excellent views of it from the coast and Compton Down), but its

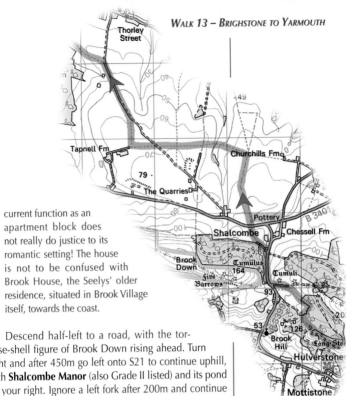

current function as an apartment block does not really do justice to its romantic setting! The house is not to be confused with Brook House, the Seelys' older residence, situated in Brook Village itself, towards the coast.

Descend half-left to a road, with the tortoise-shell figure of Brook Down rising ahead. Turn right and after 450m go left onto S21 to continue uphill, with **Shalcombe Manor** (also Grade II listed) and its pond on your right. Ignore a left fork after 200m and continue between hedgerows to a road. Cross and continue on S21, soon with a good view towards Newtown Harbour and the extensive woodland to its west.

Go through a gate (150m) and bear half-left across the field to the far corner. Shortly walk along the edge of a vast field (of rapeseed in spring), but after about 250m keep your eyes peeled for a stile on the right. Don't cross it, but take the path left across the field. Descend to cross a stream, reascend through another field, and stay in this predominantly westerly direction until a lane is reached. Take Y10 opposite and, approaching a swing gate just short of **Tapnell Farm**, strike out sharp right across the pathless grass, aiming to the right of Yarmouth, now visible, to locate a gate and turn left back on the lane. In

Map continues on page 108

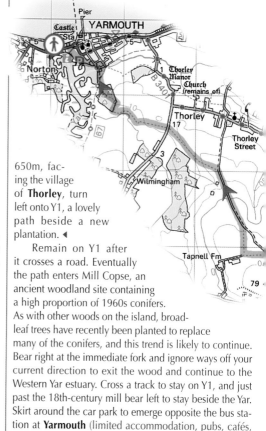

To end the walk early, continue along the lane into Thorley.

650m, facing the village of **Thorley**, turn left onto Y1, a lovely path beside a new plantation. ◄

Remain on Y1 after it crosses a road. Eventually the path enters Mill Copse, an ancient woodland site containing a high proportion of 1960s conifers. As with other woods on the island, broadleaf trees have recently been planted to replace many of the conifers, and this trend is likely to continue. Bear right at the immediate fork and ignore ways off your current direction to exit the wood and continue to the Western Yar estuary. Cross a track to stay on Y1, and just past the 18th-century mill bear left to stay beside the Yar. Skirt around the car park to emerge opposite the bus station at **Yarmouth** (limited accommodation, pubs, cafés, restaurants, shops, toilets).

WALK 14

Best of eastern Freshwater (circular)

Start/Finish	Yarmouth bus station/car park
Distance	9.8km (6.1 miles)
Grade	Easy
Time	3hrs
Refreshments	Central Freshwater (3.2km), Freshwater Bay (4.5km), Freshwater Old Village (7.2km)
Public transport	Bus route 7. **Tip** In season, bus route 21 runs early morning and late afternoon between Newport and Yarmouth via Calbourne. The buses are open-top and hugely enjoyable in fine weather. The service is under-publicised and under-used.
Parking	Car park just east of the bus station (on bend)
Early finish	Central Freshwater (3.1km, bus route 7), Freshwater Bay (4.6km, bus route 12)

This delightful and unchallenging 'figure of 8' walk is the ideal outing for day-trippers arriving on the Lymington ferry. From the charming town of Yarmouth – the smallest in the UK – the walk follows a disused railway line beside the serene Western Yar estuary, with views over to Freshwater village and Tennyson Down beyond. Beautiful Afton Marsh follows, and walkers arrive surprisingly quickly in Freshwater Bay on the opposite coast of the island, with classic views towards the mighty cliffs of High Down. Back inland, quiet paths and country lanes lead up to the old village of Freshwater, with its church, pub and quaint houses. Finally a pretty route through fields and woodland heads back onto the coastal road in Yarmouth.

From the bus station in **Yarmouth** (limited accommodation, pubs, cafés, restaurants, shops, toilets) head inland to find the car park and take footpath Y20 from its south-west corner to start the walk beside the Western Yar estuary, shortly reaching a mill.

Yarmouth Mill

The **mill** was built in 1793 to replace a 17th-century wooden one – which was itself built so that ships no longer had to continue east to Thorley on an increasingly unnavigable channel. After the Yarmouth Harbour breakwater was constructed in the 1840s the mill fell into disuse.

Just past the mill turn left on Y2 to reach what was Yarmouth station, complete with original platforms, and turn right on the former railway track to continue beside the estuary, staying on it for the next 2km. According to an information board, many of the birds that visit the Western Yar travel thousands of miles and rest here on their journey, no doubt replenishing their energy on the abundance of small sealife nesting on the mudflats. Look out too for red squirrels on the wooded bridleway. Freshwater Church can be seen in the right distance, as well as Tennyson Down and Tennyson Monument behind.

The **Western Yar** river today is just 4 miles long, but used to be much longer; the depletion of its sources over the centuries accounts for its disproportionately large estuary. The estuary – the epitome of rural tranquility – is replete with a huge array of resident and migrating birds, such as curlew, dunlin, redshank, Brent goose, teal and widgeon, and has a secure conservation status. The saltmarshes developed after Yarmouth Harbour's breakwater was built in 1847, thus slowing down the flow of the river; ongoing erosion of the marshes is a problem, however.

The track ends at a junction with a country lane beside a stone bridge: a lovely spot and the centre of the walk's figure of eight, so it will be visited again. Cross the bridge, then immediately turn left (F58). Walk through the marshland, which is potentially swampy initially. Emerging on a road, turn left at the T-junction ahead. ▸ Pass a supermarket, on the site of the old Freshwater station, to continue on Stroud Road. After 80m turn left (F37), passing through a truly idyllic garden (only the path is public, unfortunately).

Ignore path offshoots; on reaching a lane turn left, and at a T-junction go left again. After 150m turn right

Go right here for bus stops.

111

Old Newport to Freshwater railway track beside the Western Yar estuary

It is possible to end the walk here – bus stops are to the right.

beside a sign for Afton Marsh Nature Reserve (ignore the Freshwater Way signpost shortly before). Turn left at a T-junction to continue beside the marsh – another very beautiful area. Emerge onto a gravel road, and almost immediately turn left on F52, shortly turning right into a car park, now in **Freshwater Bay** (pub, café, shop, toilets). Cross the road and continue to the seafront, turning left along the sea wall. ◄

Climb the steps at the end of the sea wall and turn inland. Recross and ascend the coastal road and take the first left (Southdown Road), shortly bearing right on F32. In 250m bear left, still on F32, with the sea just visible in three directions at this junction. Keep a hedgerow on your left and bear left at the corner of the golf course (F31). At a T-junction turn right and cross the road to continue on The Causeway. Look behind for a view towards East Afton Down; on this hill in 1970, hundreds of thousands of people congregated to watch the Isle of Wight Festival, featuring Jimi Hendrix, The Doors, Joni Mitchell and numerous other A-list acts.

Soon cross the stone bridge you crossed earlier and stay on this country lane up to **Freshwater Old Village** and its church.

> The **Church of All Saints** dates from the 7th century, although it has of course been heavily restored since then, mainly in early medieval and Victorian times. The interior contains several Tennyson memorials, and several members of the family – although not the great man himself – have been laid to rest in the churchyard. The huge yew tree to the right is possibly the oldest tree on the whole island.

Take F1 beside the church wall; notice the amusing anecdote (and associated sculpture) about a drunk 19th-century smuggler! Soon pass a farm shop and café, and continue ahead on the concrete. Just before a farm driveway turn left through a fieldgate, then immediately right. Ignore path offshoots until, in 600m, the route bears right through a gate, continuing to follow the Freshwater Way.

Shortly after entering Saltern Wood turn left at a T-junction to reach a road. Here, turn right to return to the **Yarmouth** bus station via the swing bridge.

> Freshwater is, technically, almost an island itself, and at one time crossings of the Yar could be made only by ferry. A **toll bridge** linking Yarmouth and Freshwater was constructed in 1863 and was replaced with the present one in 1987. In summer it opens for 10mins every hour to accommodate vessels (they have right of way at all other times as well).

WALK 15

Best of western Freshwater (circular)

Start/Finish	Vine Inn, School Green Road, Freshwater
Distance	13.9km (8.7 miles)
Grade	Moderate
Time	5hrs
Refreshments	Colwell (2km), Colwell Bay (2.7km), Totland Pier (3.7km), Needles Park (6.7km), Dimbola Lodge tearoom (10.4km)
Public transport	Bus routes 7 and 12
Parking	Moa Place long-stay car park, School Green Road
Early finish	Colwell (1.8km), Dimbola Lodge (10.4km). Bus route 7 is always within walking distance until Alum Bay.

This walk, together with Walk 14 around the eastern part of Freshwater, offers a thorough exploration of 'Tennyson Country'. Broadly defined, Freshwater is an amalgamation of the small districts west of the Western Yar, and this walk explores several of them – such as Colwell, Totland, Freshwater Bay and the lovely hamlet of Middleton. A small part of the walk follows the Coastal Path, but mostly it is independent, and visits little-known gems such as Golden Hill Country Park, Freshwater Bay Church and the Farringford estate.

Facing the Vine Inn at **Freshwater** (limited accommodation, supermarkets, pub, limited restaurants, shops, toilets) turn right and almost immediately bear left into Longhalves. Abruptly turn left in 200m on a similar concrete path. Continue over the road, bear right, and at the first opportunity go right to enter tranquil **Golden Hill Country Park**. At the far side turn left up a broad ascending track. Take another broad track right after 200m, with views towards Freshwater Old Village, the Western Yar and the sea to the

Hatherwood Po

Chai
Alum Ba

S Old Battery

Scratchell's
Bay

Ma

south. Then take the parallel grassy path after the second bend, rejoining the track at the top. Turn left to pass the entrance to **Golden Hill Fort** (150m).

The **fort** was built as one of several Palmerston Forts to protect the Solent from French incursions, but has now found a new lease of life as an unusual conglomerate of luxury houses.

From the fort, continue on footpath F14 through woodland. Bear right at a path crossroads (300m) to reach a road in **Colwell**. Turn left, pass bus stops, and shortly turn right into Silcombe Lane. Continue past a pub, now on Colwell Lane, and at the next junction go half-right (T29/F11). Cross a road past another pub to continue on Colwell Chine Road, emerging at the sandy

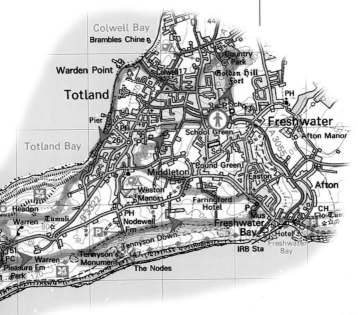

beach of **Colwell Bay**: a good swimming spot. Turn left to walk along the promenade to the privately owned pier at **Totland Bay**: built in 1879 primarily for the purpose of hosting pleasure steamers, it is currently being restored after years of neglect.

Continue until you reach a brick hut, and climb the adjacent steps. Turn right on reaching a road, and after 300m bear right on a signposted footpath. Emerging in the open after 350m, ignore a right fork to ascend **Headon Warren**. On reaching an information board (150m), break off from the Coastal Path by walking up the steep pathless hill on the left. Shortly bear right through a gap in the gorse bushes, and ascend to and cross the ridge, beside a signpost. Turn right immediately – parallel to the road below – and keep on this mainly level path, soon enjoying a commanding view over to the Needles.

Keep ignoring ways off the main path, including a left turn by a Coastal Path marker, staying near to or at the top of the ridge and eventually descending with the path on the far side of the down. Take either path at a fork, both of which will eventually lead down to a drive (just keep taking descending paths). Turn left along it, and at a junction turn right to reach the entrance to the Needles Park above **Alum Bay** (bar, cafés, restaurant, shops, toilets). ◄

Time and energy permitting, you might want to descend to the bay itself by chair lift (seasonal) or footpath.

Ascend the road to pass the car park, and turn left up steps at the first corner. Continue away from the sea on a level grassy path, ignoring ways off, which soon starts to gradually ascend. After crossing a gate in 1km you could detour up to the **Tennyson Monument** on the hill to your right. ◄ To continue, stick to the gradually descending track, soon with a view of the island's Fort Albert and the mainland's Hurst Castle.

See Walk 9.

Meet a track after 600m and continue on a path initially between bushes. Keep to the main path, and in 750m ignore a left fork into trees. Coming into open downland (650m), strike out over the pathless grass without changing direction, shortly with a wonderful view over to Freshwater Bay and the Back of the Wight. Ignore a gate in 100m and round a large stone house level with

Victorian Fort Redoubt (see Walk 9) (seaward) to reach a road next to **Dimbola Lodge**.

Thatched church, Freshwater Bay

> Victorian photographer Julia Margaret Cameron set up home at **Dimbola Lodge** after being inspired by a visit to her friend Tennyson at neighbouring Farringford. The house now hosts a permanent exhibition of her work as well as temporary exhibitions. Contemporary poet Henry Taylor remarked it was 'a house indeed to which everyone resorted for pleasure, and in which no man, woman or child was ever known to be unwelcome'. Much like today!

Turn left, past bus stops, to reach Freshwater Bay Church.

> **St Agnes Church** is the only thatched church on the island and is surprisingly modern (1908; the roof was rethatched in 1962). It was built for the benefit of Freshwater Bay residents and to ease overcrowding at All Saints at the other end of the parish. The Tennysons donated the site.

Just past the church turn left (F47). Ignore a fork on the left after 350m to continue under the charming wooden – but sadly disused – Tennyson's Bridge: it is linked to the Farringford grounds and was used by the poet for inspiration. Patrons of the accommodation and restaurant now occupying **Farringford** are welcome to use the 'secret' green door to enter the grounds. Tennyson himself used the door to visit his friend and neighbour Julia Cameron in Dimbola Lodge.

> **Farringford** was Tennyson's home from 1856 to 1867, and was host to several famous guests, such as Darwin, Garibaldi and Lewis Carroll. However, the grounds were regularly besieged by admirers, causing the despairing poet to move back to the mainland – although he did return periodically. There is self-catering accommodation and an upmarket restaurant in the grounds, and the house is currently undergoing restoration for use as a study and cultural centre.

When the track swings right, take the footpath ahead. Having descended to a road, turn right through the classy hamlet of **Middleton**, passing a couple of exquisite houses,

Witches Copse

and in 150m turn left (T7). By Stonewind Farm take the footpath ahead towards and through Witches Copse.

Turn left onto a lane and in 50m go right (T10). On entering a second field turn right along its edge, but do pause to admire the exquisite view over the rooftops of Totland towards the mainland beyond. Skirt clockwise round the next field and exit through a gap in the second corner. Turn left on the path ahead, and in 300m turn right at a path crossroads. On reaching a lane turn left, then right into Clayton Road. At its end turn left to return to the Vine Inn.

WALK 16
Shalfleet and Newtown circular

Start/Finish	New Inn, Shalfleet
Distance	10.2km (6.4 miles)
Grade	Easy
Time	3½hrs
Refreshments	None en route
Public transport	Bus route 7
Parking	Car park in Mill Road, just north of the New Inn
Early finish	No options en route, but you are always within walking distance of the main road (bus route 7)

While many places on the island offer peace, quiet and dreamy vistas, certain spots such as Niton Undercliff, on the south coast, and Newtown Harbour Nature Reserve, which is explored on this walk, have their own additional charm. The harbour is just beautiful, and perhaps the best time to visit is on a sunny, windless winter's day, when you may well have the whole harbour to yourself and hear nothing but birds. Also visited on this walk are the woodland to the east, unusually bordering the saltmarsh of the nature reserve, and Newtown itself: centuries ago it was one of the island's principal towns, and many of its grassy paths were streets back then. The National Trust is prominent in Newtown, managing the nature reserve, woods, meadows and Old Town Hall.

From the New Inn at **Shalfleet** (pub, village shop), walk down Mill Road past the car park and fork left on a stony track shortly afterwards. The track soon meets Shalfleet Lake (actually a tidal creek); continue to walk north with it, and a beautiful vista of Newtown Harbour opens up ahead. On reaching Shalfleet Quay do stop and savour the tranquility of this beautiful spot – it's hard to believe that Newtown Harbour was once a bustling port! Return on the same path, looking out for a gate on the right leading into a series of remote fields, carefully managed to balance the needs of wildlife with the practical concerns of farming. A circuit around them takes about 30mins.

Back at the original junction, take the other fork this time to continue down Mill Road, soon passing converted Shalfleet Mill, cited in the *Domesday book*. Cross over the point where the Caul Bourne feeds into Shalfleet Lake, and on reaching a road turn left. Shortly after a sign for Corf Camp turn left through a gate to follow a permissive path which soon rejoins the road. Turn left on Town Lane, and immediately after crossing a bridge over Causeway Lake (another tidal creek) turn left on footpath CB16a, initially beside the water.

Shalfleet Lake

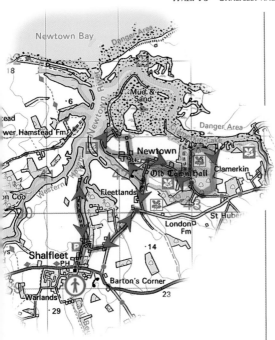

The path ascends to a lane by the church in **Newtown**, a graceful but relatively modern (19th-century) structure built on the site of a medieval chapel. Turn left along the lane, and when it ends – with remarkable dwellings on either side – continue on CB9 to enter Coastguard Meadows.

Newtown was originally known as Francheville ('Freetown') because of its freedom from patronage by the Lord of the Manor. The town was once the island's biggest settlement as well as one of its most prosperous, making its money exporting salt and oysters. However, a calamitous French raid in 1377, as well as the harbour clogging up with silt, reversed the town's fortunes irreversibly, and

121

Newport soon overtook it in importance. The town was awarded two parliamentary seats in 1584, but politics didn't keep up with social change, and the dwindling population soon resulted in the town becoming a 'rotten borough' (a constituency with a small electorate) until the Great Reform Act of 1832 disenfranchised it. Both John Churchill, first Duke of Marlborough, and subsequent Prime Minister George Canning served the constituency which, looking at the 'town' now, seems quite astonishing! The Old Town Hall, built in 1699 and maintained by the National Trust, can be visited and suggests something of the town's past status.

Oak tree in a Newtown meadow; several of the meadow footpaths were streets lined with residences in medieval times

Keeping a hedge on your left, walk round two sides of the meadow to start exploring Newtown Harbour; look for where **Newtown River** – the estuary of Shalfleet and Causeway Lakes and several other watercourses – flows into the Solent. Go through the corner gate and continue on a causeway. The serenity here, with the birdlife and bobbing boats, is wonderful.

Newtown Harbour (National Nature Reserve) is a very special place indeed. It stands at the mouth of several streams to the south, and centuries ago it was the island's principal landing area (before silting led to its decline). Today it is a profoundly peaceful and potentially therapeutic place, the very antithesis of chaotic modern life. Winter is a particularly rewarding time to visit for the experience of seeing and hearing the migrating birdlife, such as Brent geese, teal and widgeon, although a wide variety of birdlife is resident at the harbour year-round.

In 150m swing left with the causeway, ignoring the grassy path ahead. At the next path junction it is possible to detour left on another causeway (muddy and uneven) to near the harbour mouth before returning. Continue south, soon crossing a long wooden bridge, and at the end of this turn left. At a bird hide, continue back to the village lane and turn left into a narrow meadow. On reaching another lane maintain your current direction, and in 550m, with a right bend visible ahead, find a footpath on the left to enter Town Copse.

Just before the woodland path leads back out into the harbour nature reserve, turn sharp right on a path to remain just inside the wood. Keep to the current direction, occasionally straying back out into the nature reserve, until after about 500m walkers are obliged to return deeper into the wood. At a clear fork after 300m, bear right on the wider path and right again at another fork in 70m. Turn left at a T-junction with a grassy path and ignore path offshoots to emerge on a road by a Walter's Copse information board.

Turn right, and in 150m left on CB13a to walk through a series of meadows (following yellow arrows) to emerge on a lane where you turn left to reach and pass **Newtown Old Town Hall**. Descend towards the bridge over Causeway Lake (passed earlier) and continue to a T-junction. The main route from here is to return to Shalfleet the way you came: take the permissive path on the right and continue on the road when it ends, soon taking a track on your right and following it to **Shalfleet**. An alternative finish for bus travellers preferring a linear walk is to continue on CB22 opposite. In 250m branch left off the main track (in effect straight on) to eventually reach the main road. Turn left for the bus stops (buses are every 30mins).

WALK 17

Shalfleet to Newport

Start	New Inn, Shalfleet
Finish	Newport bus station
Distance	19.9km (12.4 miles)
Grade	Fairly easy
Time	6½hrs
Refreshments	Calbourne (5.8km), Porchfield (12.9km)
Public transport	*From start* Bus route 7; *from finish* Bus routes 1, 2, 3, 5, 6, 7, 8, 9 and 12
Parking	Car park in Mill Road, just north of the pub
Early finish	Newport–Yarmouth road (A3054) (10.5km, bus route 7). Sporadic bus services also serve the pub at Calbourne.

This walk starts by taking in three of West Wight's 'stalwart' villages: Shalfleet, Newbridge and notably Calbourne, with its picturesque Winkle Street and water mill (remember to bring your camera). Linking them is gentle, pretty countryside, where other walkers are likely to be few and far between. The real highlight however is magnificent Parkhurst Forest: surprisingly large and very beautiful, with a wide variety of tree life and vistas, it remains rather curiously an undiscovered treasure.

In **Shalfleet** (pub, village shop), after perhaps visiting the church, which has an early Norman tower and several interesting features, walk down Church Lane opposite the New Inn, and in 70m turn left on grassy footpath S17. Soon the Caul Bourne stream appears on the left: an occasional companion en route to Calbourne. The path eventually rises and leads onto a track (900m); merge with a track coming in from the right to continue ahead, soon with a view towards Brighstone Forest. On a left bend (300m), bear right on S35 to arrive at a road on the edge of **Newbridge**. The village, although quaint and graceful, doesn't particularly warrant a detour. Take Clay Lane nearly opposite, beside two pretty thatched cottages.

Map continues on
page 126

Turn left on S42 after 350rn. In 150m, bear right to walk through the field and into a wood, beside the Caul Bourne again. Ascend steps to a T-junction and turn right to follow a pretty path, which twists and turns through the top of the wood. At a junction, shortly after crossing the stream for the second time, it is possible to visit Calbourne Water Mill by forking left over a footbridge and continuing over the grass (a 10mins return detour).

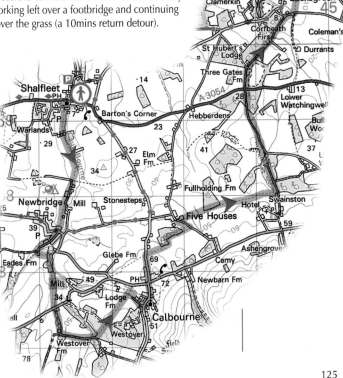

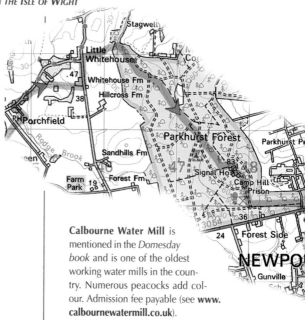

Calbourne Water Mill is mentioned in the *Domesday book* and is one of the oldest working water mills in the country. Numerous peacocks add colour. Admission fee payable (see **www. calbournewatermill.co.uk**).

Back at the junction take the other fork to continue. Cross a road to follow CB16 beside an unusual thatched bungalow. Merge with a track coming in from the right and turn left at a T-junction beside **Westover Farm**. On an ascent after 450m, look out for and follow a hidden path on the left. Once out of the wood continue towards the left of the copse ahead and cross a stile, heading in the direction of now-visible Calbourne. In 450m, having just crossed the Caul Bourne yet again, turn immediately right over the pathless grass to follow the babbling brook to and through Winkle Street, a row of lovely 18th-century cottages (some thatched) in a very photogenic setting. The street, originally called Barrington Row, has been attracting tourists for several decades.

Go left at the road ahead to walk through **Calbourne** (pub), a village in existence at least since the ninth century, and pass the 13th-century church and old village pump. Continue ahead at the Sun Inn, and after 300m ascend unmarked steps on the right which lead to a narrow footpath between tall hedgerows. Emerging in a vast field (300m), walk through it, following the yellow arrow, soon aiming for the (as yet unseen) far left corner and turning left on a lane. In 200m take CB25 sharp right. After crossing into a field, walk clockwise around it, go through a gap in the hedge on the far side and bear slightly right through the next field, aiming for the rightmost of the two hedge gaps. Once through, you have your first sight of Swainston Manor, now a hotel.

The present imposing, sumptuous building of **Swainston Manor** dates mainly from the 18th century, but a medieval chapel and hall bear testament to its days as a palace of the Bishops of Winchester, built on the site of a previous manor house dating from 735. Its name results from visits by Sweyne, Danish King of England and

Harelane Plantation

father of King Canute. Tennyson was a frequent visitor and paid tribute to the place in his poem 'In the Garden at Swainston'.

At a junction with a track go left, soon ignoring a right turn to keep ahead through the aesthetically pleasing Harelane Plantation. Cross a bridge over the old Newport–Freshwater train line to continue to the Newport–Yarmouth road (A3054) beside bus stops. ◀ Cross the road to continue on CB26; on reaching **Three Gates Farm** bear right, and in 400m bear left into a wood. Emerge on a road and turn right. In 150m turn left on hidden CB8, and on entering a second field bear right to stay near the edge. Cross a stile in the far corner to pick up CB7. Then in 100m, just after going through a gap in the fence, turn immediately left and cross a lane to continue between two back gardens, now in the village of **Porchfield** (pub).

Cross a stream, walk right then turn sharp left across a field to find a stile in its far corner. Continue past a farm to the road ahead. Detour left briefly if you fancy a pint at this point, but to continue turn right. Just before the 'Bunts Hill' road sign bear right on a very inconspicuous grassy path. Ascend the field to the far corner, then keep a hedgerow on your right and eventually reach a road. Turn left here, keeping eyes and ears tuned for traffic. Just

This is the final opportunity to break the walk.

Parkhurst Forest

after a road comes in from the left, turn right on CB5. **Parkhurst Forest** now looms ahead and walkers are soon guided into it – very much a back entrance!

> **Parkhurst Forest** is one of the oldest forests in the country according to its owners, the Forestry Commission. It is second in size to Brighstone Forest, but substantially more awe inspiring to walk through. King James I hunted here, and locals grazed flocks before the forest was enclosed at the start of the 19th century and communal rights were curtailed. Much oak planting took place subsequently to replace trees used for Nelson's navy and on former grazing land. Since 1900, periodic coniferous replanting has encouraged the island's red squirrel population, although the aim now is to increase native species while ensuring the squirrels are not driven out.

Take care to follow the directions below carefully to avoid losing your way in the forest, as other people may be few and far between. In 40m ignore a right turn. In 450m look out for and turn right through an archway to penetrate deeper into the forest. Go left at a track junction in 350m, and in 150m, where the main track swings left, carry on back into the woodland. At a T-junction (550m) go left, then almost immediately turn right at another one. In 70m turn left on a grassy path, and in 250m, at a junction beside a bench, go right. Ignore ways off until, after 250m, a crossroads with a bench on the left is reached. Turn right here and left at the first crossroads (250m) to reach privately owned **Signal House**, the highest point in the forest.

Bear right to walk around the house and remain on the concrete. Ignore all ways off and turn left at the car park. Where the drive swings right continue on the inviting path ahead, at the end of which turn right to reach the main road. Cross and turn left. By attractive Albany House (200m) turn right on N47, and on entering a field bear half-left on a faint path in the direction of Newport Minster.

Bear half-right through a second field, and at a third keep to the right-hand edge; where the edge swings right, descend half-right to a footbridge in the far corner. Emerge onto a (pleasant) estate road and turn left both here and at the T-junction. Almost immediately turn right into N47 and bear left ahead to resume the path. Turn left at the first opportunity and then right away from the supermarket. Ignore Crocker Street, but turn left into Lugley Street and take the footpath (Post Office Lane) opposite the car park. Continue up Castlehold Lane, and turn left and then right on St James Street to arrive at **Newport** bus station.

WALK 18

Gatcombe to Newport

Start	Gatcombe (turn-off for Gatcombe Church)
Finish	Newport bus station
Distance	9km (5.6 miles)
Grade	Moderate
Time	2½hrs
Refreshments	None until Newport
Public transport	*To start* Bus route 6 (ask the driver for Gatcombe bus shelter); *from finish* Bus routes 1, 2, 3, 5, 6, 7, 8, 9 and 12
Parking	The lane just beyond Gatcombe Church is possible
Early finish	Carisbrooke Castle (7.1km, bus route 6)

Starting at the overlooked hamlet of Gatcombe, with its striking medieval church and manor house, the walk soon heads west up onto remote Garstons Down. A lovely balcony path follows with distant sea views, then a brookside path meandering towards the foot of Carisbrooke Castle. The route follows two of the castle's outer walls, and the subsequent footpath provides wonderful views over Newport before the descent into the town centre.

From the bus stop, take the lane signposted 'Gatcombe' and catch glimpses of a lake on your left before arriving at **St Olave's Church**. After visiting, continue to the end of the churchyard to take a peek at the splendid 18th-century **Gatcombe House**. Back on the lane, turn left on an initially uphill path through woodland, and at a junction of paths just past cottages (650m) turn sharp right on a bridleway, soon with magisterial Tolt Copse visible to the left.

St Olave's Church at Gatcombe is a Grade I listed building built by the Estur family in the 13th century as an adjacent chapel for their property Gatcombe House (rebuilt in 1750 as a residence for the Worsley family). The church has undergone several repairs and alterations over the centuries, but the font is original and the tower 15th century. It also has the only surviving example on the island of medieval stained glass in a church (window east of the porch). The interior hosts reclining sculptures of two past owners of Gatcombe House: Sir Charles Seely in the nave (killed in action in the First World War) and (allegedly) Edward Estur to the side of the altar, whose memorial is centuries older.

Ignore a left fork after 650m and instead descend to reach a lane. Ascend in the current direction, bearing left before the entrance to Newbarn Farm. On entering a field turn left, shortly taking either of the parallel paths ahead. Continue ascending **Garstons Down**, soon with a distant sea view opening up behind. At a signpost 450m from the start of the field turn right (bridleway G22). Shortly bear right on a balcony path – it is not a widely known path

Garstons Farm

but it provides a lovely stretch of walking. Although this is approximately the centre of the island, the view potentially extends to East Cowes, the Newport–Culver downland ridge, the southeast downs and the Spinnaker Tower at Portsmouth, not to mention Carisbrooke and its castle.

Eventually the path swings right and descends to proud, solitary **Garstons Farm**. Bear left here (G7), and just before **Bowcombe Farm** turn right on N102. Turn right at a T-junction, then in 150m go left on N104 and continue with marshy Lukely Brook on the left, which flows into the Medina further along its course. Eventually cross a pretty stream and emerge onto a lane. Although you may not see it, you are just below **Carisbrooke Castle**. Turn right on this lane, then at the junction with Millers Lane continue on N88, signposted to the castle. On reaching the car park, turn left to leave it and take the path beside the castle walls (or to visit the castle walk down the road for a minute to the entrance).

> The foundations of the present **Carisbrooke Castle** were built on the site of a Roman fort by the first Lord of the Island and friend of the Conqueror, one William FitzOsbern, shortly after the Norman invasion. Fortified by his nephew Richard de Redvers, the castle served both as an important primary defence against foreign invaders and as the official residence of the island's Lords and, subsequently, Governors. It fulfilled this function until the last resident Governor Princess Beatrice's death in 1944. The castle's national claim to fame is as the site of Charles I's imprisonment for over a year before his beheading in 1649. Maintained today by English Heritage, the castle is one of the island's premier visitor attractions and is well worth a visit. Look out for the resident donkeys which for centuries have drawn water from its well!

On reaching the start of the castle's third side, immediately take the path to the left of a wooden gate, shortly crossing a road beside bus stops and taking the

Carisbrooke Castle

steps opposite. Beyond the steps the path rises gradually, soon with marvellous, ever-expanding views beside Carisbrooke cemetery, incorporating the Rowridge transmitters, Carisbrooke, Newport, the River Medina, and downs to the south.

The path descends to a suburban road; go left and take the first right (Elm Grove). Walk anti-clockwise around the playing field ahead, an attractive setting even this close to the centre of Newport. By a metal post, descend the adjacent concrete path, and at the T-junction beyond South View turn right to reach another T-junction. Go right again past characterful Nodehill Middle School (built 1904), first left into Medina Avenue, then left again to walk through Church Litten Park.

> **Church Litten Park** was once a burial ground, founded in 1582 to house plague victims, but was turned into a park by the first female mayor of Newport in 1931. Look out for the magnificent Weeping Beech tree – its melancholic quality a reminder of the park's former use.

Newport bus station is at the end of the park.

WALK 19
Tennyson Trail

Start	Carisbrooke Church
Finish	Freshwater Bay
Distance	14.9km (9.3 miles)
Grade	Moderate
Time	5hrs
Refreshments	None en route
Public transport	*To start* Bus routes 7 and 12; *from finish* Bus route 12 or the seasonal Needles Breezer to Yarmouth for a connection with bus route 7
Parking	Short-stay car park in Carisbrooke High Street; alternatively, try Priory Road
Early finish	No easy possibilities

The popular, easy-to-follow Tennyson Trail is a fantastic way of getting to the stunning Back of the Wight from Newport's neighbour, Carisbrooke. It generally keeps to ridges throughout its entire length and can be divided into three distinct parts: Bowcombe Down, Brighstone Forest, and the downland overlooking the southwest coastline. The last runs parallel to the Coastal Path way down below and heads across a landscape of ever increasing beauty and drama. Indeed, walkers may feel they are walking on air when both coastlines come into view! The trail is satisfyingly remote and encounters few man-made structures – at least until the hilltop golf course near the end. This walk ends at Freshwater Bay, which arguably is the perfect place to stop; those who have the energy to continue via the Needles to the trail's official end at Alum Bay should refer to Walk 9.

Start at the crossroads just up from the church in **Carisbrooke** (supermarket, pubs, café, restaurant, shops, toilets). Ascend Carisbrooke High Street, and in 150m bear left on Nodgham Lane. After 90m bear right uphill: the official start of the trail. Ascend gradually and continue where the path levels out just below the top of **Bowcombe Down**; the route stays at this lofty height for

135

most of the walk. Views appear and disappear, both easterly (look out for Carisbrooke Castle) and, later, north-westerly towards the mainland. If you're inspired to write poetry up here you wouldn't be alone: apparently this is where John Keats wrote the famous line from *Endymion*: 'A thing of beauty is a joy for ever'.

When you have the first view on your right (2km from the start of the trail), bear left. At a path crossroads after 1.2km, continue to stay on the ridge, with the Rowridge TV station masts still on your right. The trail eventually enters **Brighstone Forest**; ignore ways off the main track until a T-junction after a further 1.4km. Turn right, now with a wonderful view of the Back of the Wight coastline and sharing your way with the Worsley Trail.

Eventually reach a road: cross it to the right and continue, to start ascending Mottistone Down. Ignore a right fork beyond the car park and in a further 1.3km go through a gate and notice the 4000-year-old barrows (burial mounds) on the right.

The downs of the Back of the Wight were an **ancient trading route** as the shore was too inhospitable and other areas less navigable. That the Neolithic peoples chose to bury their dead on the route itself was a mark of respect.

Map continues on page 138

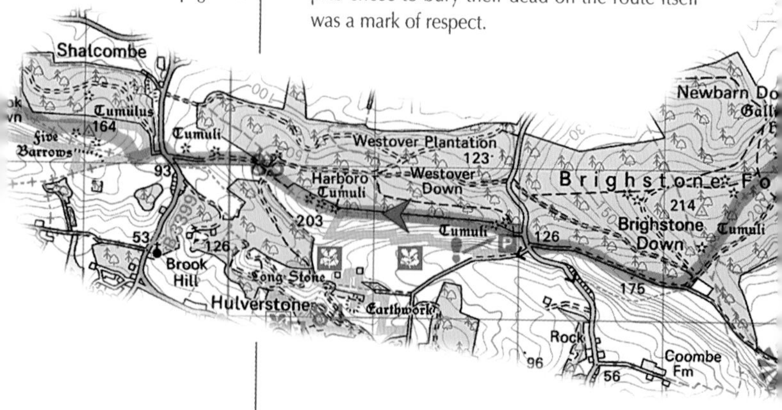

136

Continue, with an incredible two-coast panorama shortly unfolding. While descending, spot the 'white line' snaking up the hill ahead: this is your onward trail, but thankfully it's not quite as steep as it looks! On reaching a second road continue along the track opposite, shortly ignoring a branch to the left. When you feel ready, bear half-right off the chalk track to ascend the grassy escarpment, very steeply, heading towards the top of the hill. The top is known as **Five Barrows**,

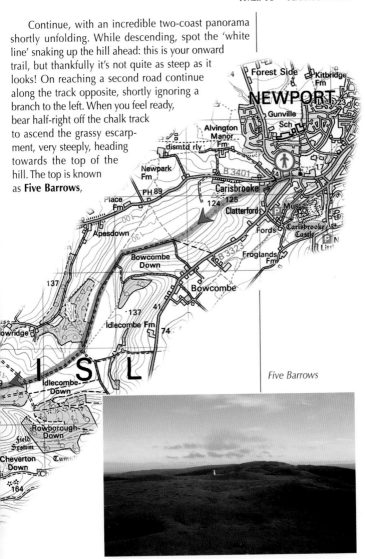

Five Barrows

View from Five Barrows towards High Down

although there are actually eight! The panoramic view is sensational.

Continue towards the chalk cliffs of High Down, eventually rejoining the path left earlier, now on a sumptuous ridge. Enter a golf course about 1.5km from Five Barrows, the northerly view opening up again and stretching from Freshwater to Newtown Harbour and Southampton beyond. In 1.3km bear left on a trail-sign-posted footpath. On reaching the coastal road turn right along it to descend to **Freshwater Bay** (pub, café, shop, toilets); bus stops are just beyond the Albion Hotel.

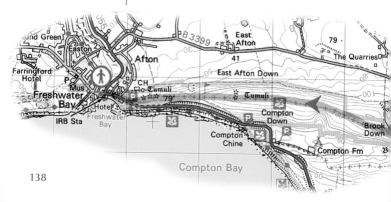

EAST WIGHT

Easterly view from Castlehaven Green (Walk 24)

WALK 20

Shanklin circular via Nettlecombe

Start/Finish	High Street, Shanklin Old Village
Distance	24.3km (15.2 miles)
Grade	Moderate to strenuous
Time	9hrs
Refreshments	Shop at the donkey sanctuary (5.8km). Although this long and sometimes strenuous walk offers almost no opportunities for refreshments, there are several places to picnic and several opportunities to cut the walk short.
Public transport	Bus routes 2 and 3, and train
Parking	Orchardleigh Road long-stay car park (off the high street)
Early finish	Whiteley Bank (5.6km, bus route 3), Dean Farm (13km, bus route 6), near Ventnor (15.7km, bus route 6), several opportunities from Ventnor cemetery to just beyond Luccombe Farm (18.6km–22.7km, bus route 3)

This walk provides a perfect introduction to the beautiful downland and coastal scenery of the island's southeast corner. There are lovely views throughout, which constantly change, and the top of St Martin's Down and the Worsley Monument are arguably the two best viewpoints on the island. The walk initially explores the downs on either side of the Wroxall valley, via a donkey sanctuary in the valley itself. The walk continues west, descending to the hamlet of Nettlecombe, and then takes an 'alternative Coastal Path' – more dramatic than the corresponding official path – high up above St Lawrence, Ventnor and finally Bonchurch before descending to the remote hamlet of Luccombe, which the Coastal Path only bypasses.

See Walk 6.

Descend the high street through the Old Village in **Shanklin** (accommodation, supermarket, pubs, cafés, restaurants, shops, toilets) and turn left beside Pencil Cottage to pass the top entrance to **Shanklin Chine**. ◄ Ignore the steps on the left to continue up to a junction, turning right on Popham Road. At the T-junction take footpath SS91 opposite – branch right in 100m, soon reaching your original road opposite Shanklin Old Church. Turn left, and in 350m left on SS8. Bear half-left with the faint path but don't continue through a hedge gap – instead keep ascending away from the road to go through a gap in a fence and continue quarter-right. Notice the view opening up behind.

Look out for and cross a stile in the treeline opposite (not the gate further right), shortly re-emerging on the main road. Turn left and, opposite a bus stop, go sharp right on SS9a, soon ascending gradually. On eventually reaching the top of **Shanklin Down**, ignore the initial junction and turn right at the T-junction just beyond (V40), soon walking on a broad grassy path with terrific views both towards the far east and far west of the island.

Keep to the main path along the ridge, bearing left with it in 600m. After a further 350m ignore a path offshoot right, and just beyond the approaching hedgerow ascend half-left over pathless grass, shortly to reach the top of **St Martin's Down** and a sweeping panoramic view. Freemantle Gate and the Worsley Monument (passed later) are visible to the north of Appuldurcombe House (beyond Wroxall).

On top of Shanklin Down

Retrace your steps to take the aforementioned path offshoot. Go through a gate to enter woodland and keep to the main descending path. At a major junction in 250m turn left (V34). Ignore ways off until the track is blocked (300m); turn right on a path through trees, and 250m later turn left through a gate to continue on

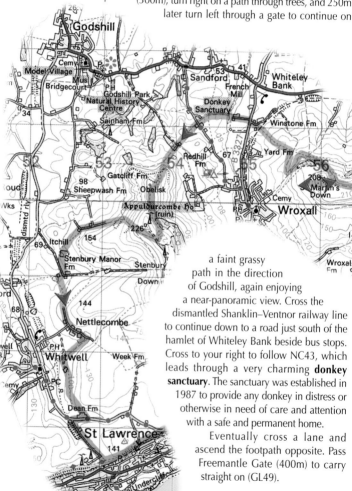

a faint grassy path in the direction of Godshill, again enjoying a near-panoramic view. Cross the dismantled Shanklin–Ventnor railway line to continue down to a road just south of the hamlet of Whiteley Bank beside bus stops. Cross to your right to follow NC43, which leads through a very charming **donkey sanctuary**. The sanctuary was established in 1987 to provide any donkey in distress or otherwise in need of care and attention with a safe and permanent home.

Eventually cross a lane and ascend the footpath opposite. Pass Freemantle Gate (400m) to carry straight on (GL49).

Freemantle Gate is a very evocative and photogenic 18th-century neoclassical folly, built as an imposing entrance to Worsley's Appuldurcombe Estate.

In a further 350m turn abruptly left (GL63) to climb very steeply up the grassy slope. About 70m beyond a

plateau of sorts bear left to head clockwise around a pit towards the **Worsley Monument** on the hill ahead. The view once you get there is possibly the most comprehensive on the island: the Back of the Wight, High Down, Carisbrooke Castle, the Solent, Culver/Bembridge Down and the suburbs of Ventnor are all visible on a clear day.

The **Worsley Monument** was erected in 1774 in memory of Sir Robert Worsley by his grandson Sir Richard (the hill was part of the Worsleys' Appuldurcombe Estate). In 1831 a lightning strike shortened it from its original 21m (70ft) height.

Map continues on page 146

Head south towards a transmitter, with Wroxall down on the left. At a path T-junction turn left. On reaching a track take GL51 to the right beyond the transmitter approach track. Just beyond the gate ahead turn right (north), in 350m crossing another (metal) gate and a wooden gate in a further 300m; then shortly turn left down a footpath in woodland. Pass farm buildings on your right after 400m, and in a further 150m follow a yellow arrow left over a stile and bear half-right towards a stile soon visible in the hedgerow on the far side of the field (stay clear of the copse to the left).

Head half-left through a second field (in the direction of St Catherine's Down) to walk beside the second side of another copse. Cross into a third field and bear half-right to exit it, turning left on the track. In 150m turn right over a footbridge. At a path junction carry straight on (GL54a). In 350m don't swing right with the field perimeter; instead turn left over stiles and immediately right to go through a gate, soon reaching a lane. Keep ahead through the hamlet of **Nettlecombe**, and when the buildings end go through a gate and descend a track, in 100m turning right (NT5) to pass three fishing lakes.

The hamlet of **Nettlecombe** was the site of a larger village in medieval times, teasingly revealed by earthworks. Perhaps one day they will be excavated and more will be learnt about the village that was. A likely reason for the decline of the village was the nationwide shift from a labour-intensive and community-focused arable economy to a more dispersed pastoral one.

At a junction with a track near the village of **Whitwell** turn left (NT12). Shortly turn right over a stile beside houses and continue through the centre of an oblong-shaped field and a second field to reach a road at **Dean Farm**, opposite the bus stop for Newport. Turn right, and after 100m go left down St Rhadagund's Path. ◄ The start of the path runs parallel to the former Merstone–Ventnor West railway line below on the right, before the

The Ventnor bus stop is obscured by bushes just beyond the junction.

latter disappears under a tunnel. When running, it was described as one of the prettiest branch lines in England.

Cross a stile in 660m to continue over the grass towards the 'High Hat' crossroads, which Coastal Path walkers will be familiar with (see Walk 7). But whereas the Coastal Path ascends from the Undercliff and continues west, this route starts its return to Shanklin by heading east. Stay on this stunning balcony path overlooking St Lawrence, but in 550m – shortly after the path heads inland – branch right down steps to a lane and ascend the other side. Turn right at the top, shortly continuing on another balcony path (although this time the view is somewhat obstructed by a hedgerow). In 250m ignore a right fork into the trees. The path shortly runs parallel to a road and eventually passes more bus stops. Shortly after, the footpath finally emerges onto the road, but in 70m look out for and ascend V64, and in a further 70m take an unmarked path left between fences to ascend **Rew Down**.

Turn left immediately past the kissing gate and, just beyond the line of bushes ahead, ascend very steeply, keeping the bushes just to your right. Soon there is a gate ahead: cross it and, against your instincts, turn left. Almost immediately turn right to climb further up the down between gorse bushes. On reaching a junction turn

View over St Lawrence

left again (the route resumes its prevalent direction near the top of the down). At a T-junction – with the Stenbury Trail – turn right, and in 250m right again to walk through the **golf course**. Keep more or less to the ridge, initially gradually ascending, and with spectacular views both south and north.

At the far end of the course pass the teeing ground for hole 11, with a sensational view towards Ventnor. Start to descend the down, and almost immediately after swinging right with the main path turn left into trees. Cross the stone wall into **Ventnor cemetery** and turn right to walk around its perimeter, soon continuing on concrete. Beside a stone lodge find and descend steps to a road. ◄

From here to Luccombe Farm the walk is never far from bus route 3, which runs along the main road at the foot of the downs.

Take Old Shute opposite and resist the tempting path leading into Old Shute Field some way along. Instead emerge on a walkway above the main road and follow it left, soon passing Ventnor Industrial Estate.

This used to be **Ventnor station**, the terminus of trains from Ryde. Walk to the far side to see a boarded-up tunnel, which is where steam trains used to emerge from deep under St Boniface Down.

After a further 300m turn left up V110 to continue just above the rooftops of Ventnor. In 350m ignore the gate ahead to bear left round the edge of the wood, ascending very steeply. The path shortly levels out and penetrates deeper through this rather dark and sinister wood. Ignore descending forks, and soon ascend even higher. Having exited the wood, the path continues up a remote section of **St Boniface Down** but swings right just before the severely steep incline. Look to your right for one of the most beautiful views of the walk: the rooftops of Ventnor have now given way to those of the quieter village of Bonchurch, a vista somewhat reminiscent of the earlier hilltop views over Ventnor's other (western) neighbour, St Lawrence.

Stay on this wonderful path, just above the houses of **Bonchurch**, until it finally meets the road again opposite a car park. Turn left, and in 150m go right (SS6), with yet another stunning view ahead. Soon descend a long flight of steps through a tunnel of trees (the steps can be slippery and in poor condition so hold onto the rail). Down in the valley cross a stile on the other side of a track to maintain your previous direction. Having reached Luccombe Farm, walk round the stone wall of the beautiful farmhouse and continue on the concrete drive.

SHANKLIN

Shanklin Chine

59

MS

Horse Ledge

Luccombe
Village

Luccombe
Bay

Luccombe Chine

en

The
Landslip

DUNNOSE

Monks
Bay

seshoe
Bay

View over St Lawrence towards a beautiful sea

At a hairpin bend, continue ahead over a stile on a grassy path. In 80m bear left, ignoring steps a little way along. ▶ Once at the hamlet of **Luccombe** take SS88 on the right, shortly continuing on a grassy footpath. When the path ends, turn left to walk through the 'main street' of the hamlet. Keep on the lane beyond it, bearing left opposite Haddon's Pits to continue back towards **Shanklin**. At the T-junction with Popham Road turn left to walk the route all over again(!) or take the descending path opposite to return via the Chine to the high street.

For bus stops take these steps to ascend back to the road.

WALK 21
Shanklin circular via Bonchurch

Start/Finish	High Street, Shanklin Old Village
Distance	9.4km (5.9 miles)
Grade	Moderate
Time	3½hrs
Refreshments	Bonchurch (5km)
Public transport	Bus route 3 (route 2 stops in Victoria Avenue, nearby, and the train station is a 10mins walk)
Parking	Orchardleigh Road long-stay car park (off the high street)
Early finish	Bonchurch (4.4km, bus route 3), top of Devil's Chimney (7km, bus route 3)

This fantastic walk explores some of the loftiest points on the Isle of Wight, on top of Shanklin, Luccombe and Bonchurch Downs. An altitude of 240m (787ft) may not sound like much, but after experiencing the views down to Bonchurch and the sea, they will doubtless stay in your memory (in mist these views can be wonderfully ethereal). Numerous steps link the three 'strata' of Bonchurch; at the lowest the walk meanders beside Bonchurch Pond and descends still further to the village's 1000-year-old church. Finally the Coastal Path is followed through the Landslip and pretty coastal fringes of Luccombe back into Shanklin.

From the bus stops midway down the Old Village high street in **Shanklin** (accommodation, supermarket, pubs, cafés, restaurants, shops, toilets), walk uphill for a short way and take the first left (Pomona Road). At the junction with Grange Road continue ahead, and where Westhill Road starts continue in your current direction (footpath SS84). Go left at a T-junction to reach a duck pond on the left and Shanklin Old Church on the right. The 850-year-old church was for centuries the private chapel of Shanklin Manor before being granted to the Old Village parish in Victorian times.

Enter the churchyard and take the footpath at the back of the church to start the ascent up **Shanklin Down**, shortly with most of Sandown Bay visible behind. Shortly after ascending a second flight of steps, the path flattens out and arrives at a signpost just after a stile. Turn left here, following the pathless field edge. Entering the next field, bear half-right to climb to the top of the hill. (In misty conditions a hollow on the left is confirmation that you are on the right track.) Reach the **trig point** at the top

View over Ventnor from Bonchurch Down

where the most glorious panoramic view awaits! On a clear day the entire width of the island from Culver Cliff to High Down is visible.

Continuing in the same direction, shortly go over two stiles and turn left, now with a peaceful lonely valley on your right, and the village of Wroxall nestling within it. Stay on this ridge-top path, soon entering Luccombe Down. About 150m before a gate leading onto a drive, branch left. Ignore ways off the main branch, shortly arriving at a stony, makeshift car park. Walk towards the bench and National Trust sign on the left, and go right on the grassy path, ignoring the spur almost immediately on your left. Head towards the glistening sea and take V42 to enter Bonchurch Down. The descent is steep, but the seascape stunning.

When the path ends, aim just to the right of the cluster of houses immediately below the precise slope you are on. Steps lead down to a road through **Upper Bonchurch**, near bus stops. Cross and turn left to almost immediately descend some (initially metal) steps, which soon carve their way through rock. Turn right at the road below, which soon becomes a footpath, and descend

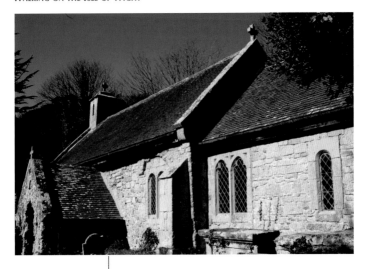

Bonchurch Old Church

via more steps to the delightful road through **Bonchurch** (limited accommodation, pub, restaurant, toilets). Turn left to pass the lovely pond (filled with carp), an upmarket restaurant and several interesting old houses. Shortly after the houses end, bear right downhill towards the 11th-century Old Church.

> **Bonchurch** is mentioned in the *Domesday book*, and its Old Church was built in 1070. Farming, fishing and quarrying were the principal occupations of the small population for centuries, the stone being exported by sea to other island and mainland locations. The village expanded rapidly in the mid-19th century, necessitating the building of a new church. But the Old Church has the charm, especially its lovely churchyard with gravestones dating to at least the early 1600s. Charles I visited the church, apparently, paying tribute at a friend's funeral, and Charles Dickens is known to have sojourned in the village while working on *David Copperfield*.

Continue descending after visiting the church: after 40m take a sharp left, now on the Coastal Path, the signs for which should be followed all the way back to Shanklin. Bear right after 30m, and opposite 'Boat House' go left to continue, following the coastline. After 350m keep straight on, ignoring steps on the left. Ignore all ways off the main path and continue through the rich broadleaved woodland of the **Landslip** (so called because of the erosion and inter- mittent landslides that have affected the area since the last ice age). After 450m, ignore footpath V65c, also known as the infamous Devil's Chimney. ▶

To cut the walk short take this path – if you don't mind climbing the 225 steps to reach the bus stops at the top.

At a junction at the top of steps (450m) turn right, soon emerging on a driveway. At a further junction (100m), take the right fork, bearing right after 200m and staying on the main path, always keeping to the same direction. After passing several secluded, beautifully sit- uated properties (part of the hamlet of **Luccombe**) and a seasonal snack bar, your goal – Shanklin – is eventu- ally seen at the forefront of the magnificent swoop of Sandown Bay.

Shortly after a road junction 300m from the snack bar, bear left off the road, but continue adjacent to it in a field, to emerge back onto it at the far right corner. Then, at the T-junction with Popham Road, continue through Rylstone Gardens, bearing left at the sculpture and pay- ing your respects to the birds in the aviary. Descend steps, pass **Shanklin Chine** (see Walk 6) – worth visiting, if not necessarily today – and continue back up to the high street.

WALK 22
Shanklin circular via America Wood

Start/Finish	Shanklin bus stands, Carter Avenue
Distance	8.2km (5.1 miles)
Grade	Moderate to strenuous
Time	3hrs
Refreshments	None en route
Public transport	Bus routes 2 and 3, and train
Parking	Shanklin station car park
Early finish	Newport–Shanklin Road (A3020) (2.8km and 7.2km, bus route 2)

This short walk offers an effective introduction to both the southeast downs and atmospheric America Wood. The final stage is particularly satisfying, making use of permissive paths near and through Holme Copse, planted by notable resident Anne Springman to form a link with Greatwood and Hungerberry Copses, its two ancient neighbours. Little-used footpaths link up with the base of Sibden Hill and Batts Copse, two areas of Shanklin greenery not usually frequented by visitors. Walkers should not tackle the latter part of this walk if fog is forecast, as careful route-finding is needed to descend from the downs.

From the bus stands at **Shanklin** (accommodation, supermarket, pubs, cafés, restaurants, shops, toilets), turn right along Collingwood Road (opposite the café), then immediately left on footpath SS15. Cross a road and soon reach Batts Copse; keep a stream on your left, and turn right when there are steps ahead and a footbridge on the left. Cross Carter Avenue and, at a T-junction ahead, turn left; turn right shortly after to cross what was once the Shanklin–Ventnor railway line and is now a track for walkers and cyclists.

Keep ahead at the next crossroads, and ahead again where the concrete ends, to find a narrow path. At the

America Wood

far side of the second field continue in the same direction, with a view of Bembridge Down slowly opening up behind. Ignore ways off your current direction, and eventually descend through trees. Opposite an isolated stone house after 600m, turn left on a path to enter **America Wood**. ▶

Stay in your current direction, but after 150m take a wide but inconspicuous path on the left (or continue on your current path to start a circuit of the wood). Turn right at a junction after 70m to descend and leave the wood. Turn left at a lane, and after 250m bear right on NC30a. Bear left on an enclosed path after 70m, which brings you to the Newport–Shanklin road (A3020). ▶ Cross and continue under a disused railway line (the same line as was crossed earlier) to start the ascent of **St Martin's Down** – the north-eastern stretch of the arc of downland centred on the village of Wroxall.

At a junction of paths after 1km go through the gate ahead and turn left just inside the wood (V46). Go through another gate (250m) and bear half-right continuing to ascend the down, still with an outstanding view behind of Sandown Bay and the Solent. On meeting a

Allegedly so called because its trees were used to build ships to fight the American War of Independence, America Wood is coniferous in parts but mainly broadleaved (notably oak).

Bus stops are to the left.

155

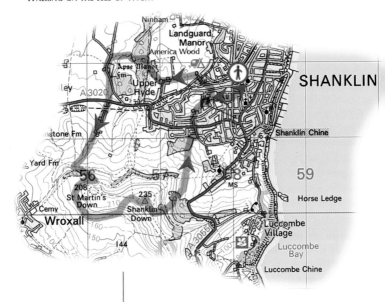

track, continue along it – look through gaps in the hedge for an uncommon view of Freemantle Gate, Wroxall, Appuldurcombe House, Stenbury Down and the Back of the Wight. Skirt round the hill on your left, ignoring ways off; then, after 750m on the track, bear left uphill on a wide, grassy path. Once at the saddle, turn right along the clear path. Perhaps pause at the forthcoming path junction to admire the stunning view north.

Keep ahead, in 100m turning left over a stile, and continue to the trig point on top of **Shanklin Down**. Start descending directly towards Shanklin on a very faint path, but just after a pit on the right (100m), turn right across the pathless grass towards a line of trees bordered by a fence. Aim for the furthest tree, to find and cross a stile. Descend with the wood on the left, soon swinging left on a clear path to enter it.

Cross a stile (70m) and continue on a very faint path towards and into Greatwood Copse ahead, shortly bearing right at a junction. In 150m turn left on a permissive path and at a path crossroads continue straight on, almost immediately bearing left towards Holme Copse.

Holme Copse was planted in 2003–4 by Anne Springman, former island High Sheriff and descendant of one of the first Lords of the Manor of Shanklin, active in the 12th century. The permissive paths are courtesy of her.

Once over the steps bear right, keeping the wood on your left, and after 150m bear left, staying with the wood. In 250m enter and quickly exit Hungerberry Copse (which counts wild cherry among its trees), and in 50m turn left down steps and descend towards a road (now back in **Shanklin**). Go left, cross Victoria Avenue (beside bus stops) and descend Chatsworth Avenue. Where the road swings right, continue ahead on SS99 and keep to the right of the wood (although Sibden Hill is worth a detour: take one of the left branches). Eventually, descend steps to the crossroads in Batts Copse, which was passed at the start of the walk. Go straight across and follow the paths back to the bus stands.

View from Shanklin Down

157

WALK 23
Shanklin to Godshill

Start	Shanklin station
Finish	Godshill
Distance	7.4km (4.6 miles)
Grade	Fairly easy
Time	2½hrs
Refreshments	None en route
Public transport	*To start* Train and bus route 3 (bus route 2 stops nearby); *from finish* Bus routes 2 and 3
Parking	Station car park
Early finish	Apse Heath (2.8km, bus route 8)

This short and easy walk makes for a pleasant half-day ramble between Shanklin, a popular resort on the east coast, and Godshill, one of the island's idyllic honey-pot villages. Make sure to leave time to look around Godshill: stroll up to the beguiling 15th-century church, see the model village, have tea in a quaint café, and mingle with more 'mainstream' tourists – who probably won't be encountered on the walk itself, even at the lovely secluded ponds at Ninham.

Facing the station at **Shanklin** (accommodation, supermarket, pubs, cafés, restaurants, shops, toilets) turn left and walk down the steps, turning right at the bottom. After 60m take bridleway SS18. Reaching a T-junction at a holiday home area turn right. Soon walk through a pretty park (ignore the adjacent gate), exiting at the far right corner and turning left. After 450m a right turn leads to the ponds at **Ninham**, a pleasant place to picnic. Swing right after the larger pond, soon ascending a broad woodland track. Where the track levels out briefly, look down to the left for a comprehensive view towards America Wood.

Pond at Ninham

Just before reaching the barn visible ahead, turn right (NC29) and left by the pumping station. ▶ Soon cross a road and continue on NC28, shortly alternating left and right; at the far side of a field behind a solitary house, turn left following the yellow arrow. Cross the next road and continue, shortly enjoying near-panoramic views and Godshill visible on the horizon.

If you want to end the walk, continue ahead at the pumping station until the road at Apse Heath for bus stops.

Map continues on page 160

SHANKLIN

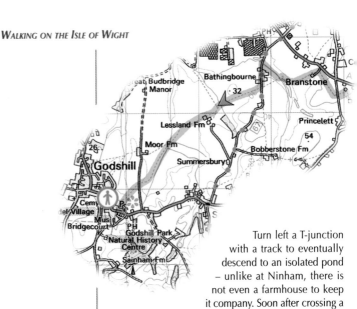

Turn left a T-junction with a track to eventually descend to an isolated pond – unlike at Ninham, there is not even a farmhouse to keep it company. Soon after crossing a plank-bridge turn left and bear right just before crossing the stream to enter a dainty, grassy little section. Keep the stream on your left – when a road takes its place find the gate which leads down onto it and turn left through the hamlet of **Bathingbourne**, perhaps pondering the fact that somewhere as apparently insignificant as this was mentioned in the *Domesday book*.

After 350m turn right (GL28), with the Chillerton and Rowridge transmitters coming into view and, eventually, Godshill Church. After 1.3km, or 90m before gates bar your way, locate and follow an indistinct path off to the right with a footbridge ahead. On meeting a track follow it right, then almost immediately branch off left to stay beside the fence, with Godshill Church (but not the village) now prominent. Start bearing right towards the end of the field and keep to the right of the next. On meeting a track continue on the path opposite. The view from the top of the incline reveals the church lording over now-visible **Godshill** (pubs, cafés, shops, toilets). Descend and continue through the village car park to reach the high street.

WALK 24

Niton circular via The Undercliff

Start/Finish	Niton village centre (Norris Grocery)
Distance	6.5km (4.1 miles)
Grade	Moderate
Time	2hrs
Refreshments	Buddle Inn (2.3km and 5.3km)
Public transport	Bus route 6
Parking	Use of the youth club car park is permitted (Star Inn Road)
Early finish	Outskirts of Niton (5.6km, bus route 6)

St Catherine's Lighthouse is seen in its spectacular glory from the Coastal Path, but detours are seldom made down the cliffs, either to the lighthouse or the surrounding secluded village of Niton Undercliff, with its almost Mediterranean feel. This exquisite walk does just that. In winter, if the island is invaded by biting northerly winds, the shelter provided by the cliffs to the north makes this the walk to do! And choose a sunny day to capitalise on the sea views, some of which are among the best on the island. This walk can be combined with Walk 25; both have the same start/finish point.

From the grocery store at **Niton** (pub, food shops, toilets) walk along Church Street opposite Rectory Road, shortly passing the church and source of the Eastern Yar on the right. Where the road bends left 300m from the church, turn left onto footpath NT33. Cross two stiles and marvel at the sea ahead – due south. At a T-junction go right, now on the Coastal Path. After 650m, by a bench and signpost and with a breathtaking seaward view, descend very steeply left on a magical little footpath, the foliage providing a marked contrast to the relative bareness of the cliffs.

Reach a lane at the bottom of the path, once part of a road to Blackgang before becoming a victim of erosion. Turn left, now in dreamy Niton Undercliff. Turn right at a road, and right again after 70m. ▶ After 500m continue on a gravel track into the **Knowles Farm Estate** (owned by

Alternatively, you may wish to detour left at the second junction to the 16th-century Buddle Inn (100m) (there is another opportunity to visit later).

161

the National Trust). Guglielmo Marconi conducted early wireless experiments behind the farmhouse in 1900, and the base of a communication mast can still be seen.

> **Niton Undercliff** is the island's most southerly village. Truly idyllic and under-explored (perhaps due to its relative inaccessibility), it developed into a proper community only in Victorian times, and it forms the western extremity of the wider Undercliff, which stretches to Ventnor. Its lush vegetation is testament to its warm microclimate, and certainly it possesses a very special ambience. Marconi stayed and worked at the Royal Sandrock Hotel (near the Buddle Inn), which sadly burned down in the 1980s.

Continue past the farm, now a holiday cottage, on a 'grass carpet', and meander down to the sea. The effects of erosion are all too clear here. It is possible to detour over the stile in the corner to explore, but the onward route is to turn left, following a path of sorts along the cliff edge. On reaching the perimeter wall of **St Catherine's Lighthouse** walk around its three navigable sides and continue, still following the coastline. At a T-junction turn left (or make the short detour right to rest or picnic at Castlehaven Green). Bend right with the lane, with marvellous sea views all the while. Find a romantic little garden on your right 350m after the bend, with a

Cottages, Niton Undercliff

well-situated bench facing the sea – an apparently public and truly idyllic little spot.

View towards St Catherine's Lighthouse

> Located on the island's southerly point and commissioned after the notorious *Clarendon* shipwreck in 1836, **St Catherine's Lighthouse** went into operation in 1840 to replace a 14th-century warning light and the defunct lighthouse on top of St Catherine's Hill, known as the Pepper Pot. The new lighthouse was somewhat revolutionary in design and produced a particularly powerful light by contemporary standards (its current range is 26 nautical miles). Tours take place at certain times of the year.

At a T-junction turn left for a first or second visit to the Buddle Inn – but the onward route is right. At the next T-junction, unless the path opposite has been reopened, turn left, passing bus stops on the bend, and 300m from the junction turn right. At the next junction take the left fork; and at a six-path junction after 400m, continue ahead (the second path clockwise). Ignore ways off, and on reaching a road turn left to return to the grocery store at **Niton**.

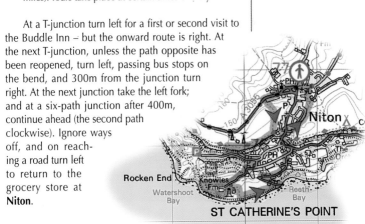

WALK 25

Niton circular via St Catherine's Down

Start/Finish	Niton village centre (Norris Grocery)
Distance	8km (5 miles)
Grade	Moderate
Time	2½hrs
Refreshments	None en route
Public transport	Bus route 6
Parking	Use of the youth club car park is permitted (Star Inn Road)
Early finish	Near Blackgang (7km, bus route 6)

A great little hike which can easily be combined with the other Niton round-walk (Walk 24) near the end. Whereas the latter explores the undercliff below Niton, this walk treads the downland above it, specifically little-known Head Down and the much more popular St Catherine's Down, which hosts the Hoy Monument and St Catherine's Oratory Lighthouse, also known as the Pepper Pot. Grand vistas abound.

From the grocery store at **Niton** (pub, food shops, toilets) walk along Church Street opposite Rectory Road. Just before the church turn right onto Pan Lane, and 300m further turn right again on footpath NT54 to walk through Ladyacre Farm. Once past it, ascend left towards a fieldgate on the lower slopes of **Head Down**. Keep a fence on your right in the next field: Niton is visible to the right, and the village of Whitwell and hamlet of Nettlecombe ahead. Walk round two sides of this field; midway along the second side look out for and cross a stile onto a short, pretty path. Turn left at the T-junction, then almost immediately right over a stile, again keeping the field edge on your right. The glorious near-panoramic view is worth savouring. Downcourt Farm, visible below St Catherine's Down, will be passed soon.

Cross a stile to steeply descend the next field. Start descending a third field, but bear half-left (off path) near the end to cross a gate beside an isolated thatched residence. March straight across the pathless grass to cross a stile into a vast field. Keeping to the same direction, in about 300m and when nearly level with a metal gate over on the left, bear half-right to locate and cross a less conspicuous gate. Head towards and pass **Downcourt Farm** (currently let year-round as holiday accommodation), and just beyond the farmhouse turn left up a grassy bank. Immediately past a wooden gate (250m) turn sharp right along a lovely balcony path, complemented by stretches of gorse.

On reaching a stone wall ascend the escarpment, shortly bearing right to scramble to the top – where you detour right to reach the Hoy Monument. ▶ Retrace your steps briefly, but continue along the ridge. In about 600m, beside a post with blue arrows, take either fork, then on reaching a gate bear half-left and turn right at a fence to ascend **St Catherine's Hill** and eventually reach **St Catherine's Oratory Lighthouse**. After admiring the sensational vista, bear half-right towards the sea, shortly with a view down towards Blackgang Chine.

Beyond a gate, bear half-left towards the higher and smaller of the two car parks visible. Having descended to the point where the slope becomes prohibitively steep, turn left on a faint path. To end the walk here by taking the bus towards Newport, turn right when level

See Walk 11 for the history of the Hoy Monument, and of St Catherine's Oratory Lighthouse (see below).

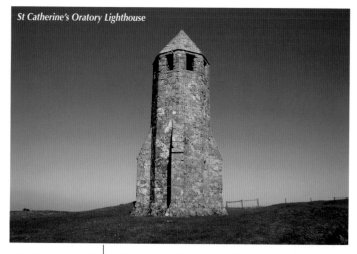

St Catherine's Oratory Lighthouse

For the bus towards Ventnor, turn right to reach the road and bus stop.

with the car park to find the bus stop on the other side of the road. Continue to a T-junction with a concrete drive. ◄

Turn left and immediately right (NT52), with Niton soon coming back into view. Eventually you reach the road. ◄ If it's still early and you have the energy you may wish to undertake the Niton via The Undercliff walk (Walk 24), in which case cross the road to take NT33 and follow the walk directions. Otherwise, turn left, passing the source of the Eastern Yar, to return to the centre of **Niton**.

For a Newport-bound bus stop turn right, and for a Ventnor-bound bus stop turn left.

Source of the Eastern Yar, Niton

WALK 26
Ashey station circular

Start/Finish	Ashey station; alternative start/finish: Newchurch
Distance	12.6km (7.9 miles)
Grade	Moderate to strenuous
Time	4½hrs
Refreshments	Newchurch only
Public transport	Steam train to Ashey. Newchurch is accessible by the seasonal Downs Breezer from Ryde. In July/August 2013, the first train from Wootton arrives at Ashey at 10.35am, with the last train returning at 4.20pm. If you miss the last train, walk north to Ashey village and call for a taxi.
Parking	Newchurch car park (Ashey station is accessible only to pedestrians)
Early finish	No alternatives besides Ashey station and Newchurch

Ashey station must be one of the quaintest and most pleasantly located stations in England and is the perfect place to start a country walk. Fit walkers could take the train from Wooton to Ashey (make sure you tell the guard that you wish to alight at Ashey) and complete the walk in time to take a return trip on the railway. Drivers, or those who wish to take their time, are advised to start at Newchurch. Wherever you start, this is a lovely walk best done when the trees are in leaf. Highlights are the charming village of Newchurch, Ashey sea mark, and the most delightful woodland views on the island.

Exit **Ashey station** and turn right at the track.

In 1966 the **Ryde to Cowes railway line** was one of the final victims of the dismantling of the island's network, but five years later, and after much effort, the Wight Locomotive Society made the Smallbrook Junction to Wootton section – of which Ashey is part – open to the public as a heritage railway, and trains have been running on the line ever since.

Ashey station

See Walk 33.

Keep ahead where it crosses the railway line to walk around the western boundary of what was once Ashey Racecourse. Opened in 1884 and burned down in 1929, in its heyday the racecourse attracted 3000 spectators for its thrice-annual meets and even had its own railway station.

Aim for and cross the road in the distance to take the footpath nearly opposite; turn right and almost immediately ascend three flights of steps up **Ashey Down**. Continue ascending beyond the steps, and when the **sea mark** comes into view cross a stile towards it. ◄ After admiring the sensational panoramic view, turn right and continue on a faint path through the grass. Turn left on reaching a road and immediately left again on Brading Down Road, keeping to the grassy verge. In 100m follow footpath NC3 over a stile, and almost immediately bear right on a faint path parallel to a fence just above it, with an exceptional view south and southwest.

Having passed a trough in 350m, descend three-quarters-left to locate and cross a stile hidden in a fence. Turn left at the track below, which narrows to become a long but very pleasant path through this tranquil side-valley.

On finally reaching a T-junction turn right. Cross the Bembridge Trail (950m) to continue on NC10, and in 450m ignore B53 branching left. A boardwalk soon leads over the boggy ground. Turn right at a T-junction with the concrete Yar River Trail (with the Eastern Yar on the left) and continue to the road at **Newchurch** (pub).

Turn left to walk up the hill towards the village centre. Shortly take NC11 running parallel to the road and look out for steps on the right that ascend to the churchyard. The village is beyond, but the onward route is to turn left to follow the churchyard wall. At the far end, return to and continue on your original path, but almost immediately turn right on a permissive footpath through a plantation, and in 100m turn left on a clear path. In a further 150m keep to your current direction, now on the right edge of the plantation, and at a fork in a further 110m bear right into woodland. At the top of a rise turn left through **Hill Farm** and in 200m descend left into a beautiful wood.

Ignore a left turn after 200m and another path offshoot after a further 200m. In a further 150m, bear left back into the open and continue towards and through a gate visible below. Shortly meet the Yar River Trail again and

Eastern Yar at Alverstone

take B54 opposite, beside the Yar. Shortly after crossing the river by lovely Alverstone Mill, turn left at the lane to walk through **Alverstone**. In 150m keep ahead, soon branching off on a bridleway to keep maintaining the same direction. Ascend to the road over the downs; the gradient keeps increasing, but so does the scope of the vista towards Sandown Bay. Turn left at the road, with the view now north and west.

In 550m turn right to descend into Bloodstone and Eaglehead Copses.

> To all intents and purposes **Bloodstone and Eaglehead Copses** form one wood, and ancient woodland at that. Oak, ash and hazel are predominant and, as with much of the island's woodland, coppicing is practised, which increases nut production for the benefit of the red squirrels. Tits, owls and buzzards may also be seen.

Take the right fork at a junction after 700m, in a further 300m bear left to enter another wood, and immediately bear left again to continue along the edge of a field.

Look out for and follow a hidden left turn after 150m, cross a steam, and continue towards a track. Turn right here to a road and take R29 almost opposite to return to **Ashey station**. ▶

Remember that Ashey is a request stop, so hold out your hand to stop the train!

WALK 27
Ryde to Ventnor

Start	Ryde Pier
Finish	Ventnor
Distance	26.3km (16.4 miles)
Grade	Initially easy, but the walk becomes progressively harder; the final ascent onto Wroxall Down is strenuous
Time	9hrs
Refreshments	A sprinkling of possibilities between Ryde and the pub at Pondwell (3.4km); thereafter only Brading (8.7km) and Wroxall (22km)
Public transport	*To start* Bus routes 2, 3, 4, 8 and 9, and train; *from finish* Bus routes 3 and 6
Parking	Long-stay car parks in St Thomas Street, just west of the pier
Early finish	Pondwell (3.4km, bus route 8), Brading (8.7km, bus routes 2 and 3), Newport–Lake road (A3056) (17.1km, bus route 8), Newport–Shanklin road (A3020) (19.6km, bus route 2), Wroxall (22km, bus route 3)

This walk is perfect for Portsmouth daytrippers who want to attempt a challenging coast to coast walk with continued interest and variety. But if the distance is likely to be too demanding, then Brading – home of the island's oldest house and several other curios – makes a convenient place to split the walk. As ever, the main draw is the scenery: views are simply stunning on top of Brading Down, and even more so from St Boniface Down on the descent to Ventnor. But the sheer variety of landscape is also an enticement, ranging from the initial Coastal Path section to lonely fields and centuries-old farms between Pondwell and Brading, picturesque bluebell woods alive with birdsong, and the final dramatic downland finish.

From the pier at **Ryde** (accommodation, supermarket, pubs, cafés, restaurants, shops, toilets), head east along the esplanade and keep to the seafront at the fork. Aim for **Appley Tower** in the distance, and at the junction beyond it bear left to continue along the sea wall. At Puckpool Park, keep to the sea wall or take a path through the park. Continue along the seafront beyond the Boat House pub, now in **Spring Vale**, a 'suburb' of Seaview.

Turn inland at the first opportunity (Oakhill Road), and by the entrance to Seaview Wildlife Encounter turn left on footpath R59. On reaching a road in **Pondwell**, by the Wishing Well pub and bus stops, turn left, and after 150m turn right on R61. Having rounded an enclosure, possibly with resident horse and chickens, cross a field and turn left at a T-junction, now on a wide track. Pass through rustic **Park Farm**, and 500m later go straight across a track onto B11, continuing to enjoy the quiet and solitude. Look behind for your last view of the Solent – at least for now!

Continue towards and through **Hill Farm**, with Brading and Sandown Bay soon visible ahead, and descend to a road. Turn left and walk (carefully) for 400m, then turn

Brading

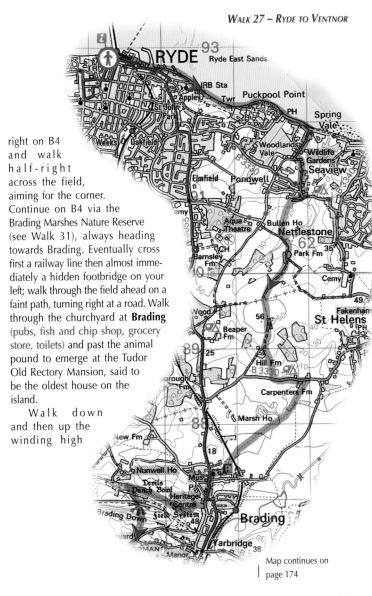

right on B4 and walk half-right across the field, aiming for the corner. Continue on B4 via the Brading Marshes Nature Reserve (see Walk 31), always heading towards Brading. Eventually cross first a railway line then almost immediately a hidden footbridge on your left; walk through the field ahead on a faint path, turning right at a road. Walk through the churchyard at **Brading** (pubs, fish and chip shop, grocery store, toilets) and past the animal pound to emerge at the Tudor Old Rectory Mansion, said to be the oldest house on the island.

Walk down and then up the winding high

Map continues on
page 174

173

For those who wish to end the walk here, bus stops are situated where the main road swings left.

street. ◄ Walk up the secondary road ahead (The Mall). In 100m turn right into a surgery car park and continue into the playground. Then immediately turn left uphill, a lovely scene of newly planted trees and (perhaps) wildflowers, and a delightful view back towards Brading – and Hill Farm which was passed earlier. Go through a gap in the treeline and turn right on the path beyond. Stay on the main, undulating path ignoring ways off. You are now walking on Nunwell Down: rich, broadleaved ancient woodland and a joy to walk through.

After 1.3km – or 150m before a junction with a three-way signpost – bear sharp left on a wide path, ascending and going back on yourself. Go through a gate near the top to leave the wood and swing right with the main path to cross the road at the top of the down – after admiring

Map continues on page 177

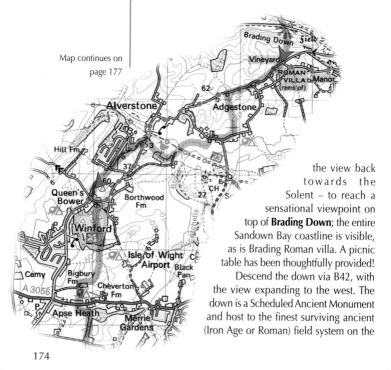

the view back towards the Solent – to reach a sensational viewpoint on top of **Brading Down**; the entire Sandown Bay coastline is visible, as is Brading Roman villa. A picnic table has been thoughtfully provided! Descend the down via B42, with the view expanding to the west. The down is a Scheduled Ancient Monument and host to the finest surviving ancient (Iron Age or Roman) field system on the island. In 200m turn right at a junction of paths to continue the descent through a wooden gate. Shortly ignore steps on the left, and turn right on reaching a road, now in **Adgestone**, or more specifically beside Adgestone vineyard, reputedly Roman and the oldest in Britain.

Stay on this very quiet and pleasant lane for 800m then, on the brow of a hill, turn left on B44. Having descended to another quiet lane turn right. Then just after 'Highleigh' on the right (300m), take B51 left. Coming into the open, keep the field boundary on the right initially, then swing left to cross in succession two streams, the Eastern Yar and a track which was once the railway line from Newport to Sandown and is now part of the Yar River Trail.

At the next junction – opposite a sign for Skinners Meadow – turn right, and in 100m turn right again through Alverstone Mead Nature Reserve (look out for the wildlife hide at the start of the path).

> **Alverstone Mead Nature Reserve** is home to dragonflies, kingfishers, woodpeckers, herons, barn owls and a host of other fauna. Red squirrels may also be spotted in the ancient woodland.

A long boardwalk soon leads out onto a lane near **Alverstone**. Take a short detour right to see the pretty

Alverstone Mead Nature Reserve

175

Eastern Yar flow through the hamlet; otherwise cross the lane and continue on NC42, branching off the track in 250m. Reach and cross a lane to continue on NC4. At the lane through the hamlet of **Queen's Bower** – named after the last Lord of the Isle of Wight, Lady Isabella de Fortibus – turn left, in 80m descending an unmarked footpath into Borthwood Copse. ◀

At a crossroads in 150m, turn right slightly uphill. Stay on this main path, ignoring all ways off your current direction (which is nearly due south). After 600m exit the wood completely and come out into the open to continue on a broad grassy path. Keep ahead at a four-armed signpost and turn right at the field corner. Cross a drive and take the narrow path ahead that emerges on the Newport–Lake road (A3056) with bus stops nearby. Descend NC37 opposite, through another delightful stretch of woodland.

At a crossroads (700m), continue on NC37 through a field, with America Wood below and the downland still to climb beyond. Descend steps into more woodland, and after a potentially boggy stretch officially enter **America Wood**. ◀ At a junction 70m from the barrier, turn right on a narrow path to start a semi-circuit of the wood's northern half. In 500m ignore a right turn, and shortly afterwards – at a wooden barrier with a stone house ahead – turn right along a wide track through the southern portion of the wood.

Stay on this main track, eventually emerging on the Newport–Shanklin road (A3020) (closest bus stops to your right), and take NC39 opposite. Cross the disused Shanklin–Ventnor railway line to continue over a stile. Cross a second stile (150m) and a third immediately on your right to ascend half-left over the pathless grass, aiming for the crest of the hill just to the right of the trees ahead (a steep, strenuous climb, but with a wonderful view now behind you).

After crossing three stiles bunched together, continue just 40m to the foot of the hillock ahead, and turn right on a faint level path. On entering another field, keep ahead on the main, level path. Keep to the left of a fence (150m),

Borthwood Copse, a corruption of 'Broadwood', is the first of a series of bluebell-carpeted woods south of Alverstone, most likely a surviving part of ancient hunting forest.

Allegedly so called because its trees were used to build ships to fight the American War of Independence, America Wood is coniferous in parts but mainly broadleaved (notably oak).

cross a stile (350m) and turn left to enter a wood. Continue at the crossroads along V34, and in 200m, with a view of Appuldurcombe House in the valley ahead, bear left onto an unmarked wide grassy path. Gradually descend and ignore ways off. On reaching a small green facing the church at **Wroxall** (grocery store, pubs), bear left. ▶

Continue into St Martin's Road, and in 100m turn right on a concrete path, continuing on grass just past the playground. Once over a stream, ignore ways off for 250m then, just after a third metal gate, turn left uphill. Swing right with the track; after 150m go through another gate and turn right along a pretty grassy path with lovely wildflowers in spring. Reach Wroxall Cross near a bridge over the disused Shanklin–Ventnor railway line. Turn left to take a private road (not Middle Barn Lane), and continue on a drive after 40m (V8) to start the increasingly steep climb up Wroxall Down, with a particularly pleasant wooded section near the top.

Alternatively, for refreshments or to shorten the walk, continue over the bridge to the main road and bus stops.

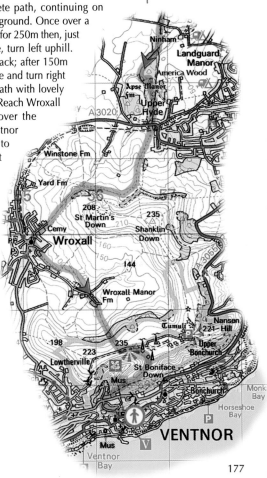

177

Wood on Wroxall Down

Technically the island's highest point is at the nearby radar station: 241m (791ft) above sea level.

On eventually reaching the ridge turn left along the drive, and after 150m turn right on V1a. ◄ At the end of the path, facing the shimmering sea, turn right onto V1 to commence the most spectacular section of the walk. In 200m, where the more obvious path curves clockwise, continue ahead over the grass, keeping the sea to your left and a steep-sided valley to your right; the outskirts of Ventnor can be seen nestling in the greenery ahead.

After a while descend steeply, soon finding steps. At the bottom of the slope descend more steps, eventually emerging in an industrial estate that was once Ventnor station. Turn left at the road for bus stops (route 3) or, to continue to the town centre, descend Grove Road opposite and take the first right (Tulse Hill). Emerge at the bus stop on the high street in **Ventnor** (accommodation, supermarket, pubs, cafés, restaurants, shops, toilets), but if you wish to take 'coast to coast' literally continue another few hundred metres to the seafront.

WALK 28

Seaview circular

Start/Finish	Centre of Seaview (St Peter's Church)
Distance	18.1km (11.3 miles)
Grade	Moderate
Time	6hrs
Refreshments	St Helens (2.4km), Bembridge Down (8.1km), Bembridge Point (13.6km)
Public transport	Bus route 8
Parking	Car park in Pier Road (en route)
Early finish	St Helens (2.4km, bus route 8), foot of Gander Down (6.5km, bus route 8), Whitecliff Bay (10km and 10.9km, bus route 8), Bembridge Point (13.6km, bus route 8)

Some of the island's hidden gems (or at least hidden to tourists) are revealed on this greatly rewarding walk. The overlooked village of Seaview has some of the most interesting residence exteriors on the island, especially by the shoreline. Beyond is St Helens which, uniquely for the island, is centred around a village green, apparently the second-largest in England. The relatively low height of Gander Down belies the rare view of Brading from its summit, while Bembridge and Culver Downs provide sensational views of Sandown and Whitecliff Bays. A walk through pretty Steyne Wood brings you to a windmill (National Trust) on the outskirts of Bembridge, after which the official Coastal Path is followed, slightly inland, back to Seaview.

From the bus stops beside the church at **Seaview** (limited accommodation, pub, cafés, restaurants, shops, toilets), start walking round the church and turn right into Madeira Road heading towards a small parade of shops. Cross the crossroads to pass the car park and descend towards the sea. Choose either route at the fork: they will merge again shortly and you will eventually arrive on the shoreline at Seagrove Bay. Walk a few paces seaward for

the view then return to ascend steeply, shortly passing some intriguing properties.

Pass the entrance to the **Priory Bay Hotel**, go over a stile, and continue along the left side of a field. On walking through a second field, notice the tower of St Helens Church peeking through the trees on your right.

> Unusually isolated for a parish church, **St Helens Church** was built in 1717 to replace its recently disused predecessor by the sea (passed on Walk 2). In those days the parish included what is now Seaview and even eastern Ryde. The church was almost completely rebuilt in the 1830s.

At a road cross to the right and continue on footpath R82. Ignore a right fork in 500m to emerge opposite the village green of **St Helens** (pub, restaurants, shops, toilets).

> **St Helens** has its origins in Saxon times, when it was probably called Etharin. Originally centred on the area known as the Duver ('duver' is an island word for sand dunes), a wooden church was constructed there in the eighth century but destroyed in 998. Then in the 1080s a Benedictine Priory, dedicated to St Helena, was established approximately where today's Priory Bay Hotel stands. A French invasion was repelled in 1340, and six years later it was from here that Edward III left to successfully invade Normandy. Nelson too departed from St Helens, for the Battle of Trafalgar, and it is said that the village was his last view of England. The village green is a conservation area – the cottages are mainly 18th century and very few properties have been built since the Second World War.

Turn right on the road and keep to this direction until the bottom of the hill. Just after the pavement ends turn left on B56 along the disused Bembridge–Brading railway branch line (known as Laundry Lane), which soon enters Brading Marshes Nature Reserve (see Walk 31). ▶

The railway was in operation from 1882 to 1953, and ran frequent trains between Bembridge and Brading, which called also at St Helens.

When the track eventually ends go through a gate onto a path (1.3km). Emerging onto a lane turn left on B3 keeping the hedge on your left and cross one branch of the Eastern Yar (350m), followed by another (150m). At a junction almost immediately afterwards take the right fork, go through a gate and ascend Gander Down (ahead) to the top where, despite being just 39m (128ft) high, there is a marvellous panoramic view, including a rather special view of the houses of Brading, nestling on a hillside. Notice Brading station below the church.

From the top, head directly towards Bembridge Fort (on top of the hill to your right as you face the sea). Soon gates should be seen below: aim for and cross them, and cross the road ahead to take BB44. ◄ Bear half-left to steeply ascend **Bembridge Down** (no path); there's no hurry to reach the ridge, but always keep ascending towards it. Once at **Bembridge Fort**, skirt clockwise around it, the view now towards Ryde, St Helens, Bembridge Airport and Harbour, and a swathe of the mainland's south coast.

> **Bembridge Fort** is a 'Palmerston Folly', built in the 1860s in response to a perceived threat of French invasion. It served a more practical purpose during the Second World War as home to an anti-aircraft unit and local headquarters of the Home Guard. The National Trust purchased the fort in the 1960s.

Head towards the Lord Yarborough Monument (see Walk 1) when it becomes visible (still staying on the ridge), eventually being led onto a drive. Turn left then almost immediately right, through the hedge, to keep following the ridge on grass, now back with the magnificent view of Sandown Bay. After being led back onto the drive, walk past the monument (to be revisited later) and the **Culver Haven Inn** (which could be immensely useful in adverse weather). ◄

Descend to Culver Battery (another fortification, completed in 1906) and ascend the grass opposite (now on the **Culver Down** peninsula), heading for

Bus stops are 5mins walk to the right.

The information board just past the pub states that the first wireless signal station on the south coast was erected here in 1900.

the sea, until a protective fence prevents any further progress. Turn left to follow the fence in the direction of Whitecliff Bay. Reaching a corner, with a fantastic view of the eroded Whitecliff Bay cliffs, bear sharp left on an ascending faint grassy path. Keep to your current direction, with the fence always nearby on your right. Go through a gate and bear left back towards the **Lord Yarborough Monument**.

On top of Culver Down looking towards Bembridge

When there – or when level with the Culver Haven – descend the slope, still heading away from Whitecliff Bay, soon to find and follow a stony path descending the down. Ignore ways off to reach Glovers Farm. A further 200m along the lane turn right abruptly on BB17. ▸ At a T-junction inside a holiday park turn right, keeping a fence on your right, and walk round the holiday homes. Turn left just past the crazy golf course and at a cross-roads of sorts continue in the same direction to keep the majority of holiday homes on the right.

Alternatively, continue to the end of the lane to find bus stops.

In 70m branch into woodland, and at the end of the path turn left to reach the road. ▸ Turn right and, in

Bus stops are on the left.

183

Frosty scene in Steyne Wood

250m, left (BB22), soon entering Steyne Wood, a relatively untouched area of ancient woodland. Cross the next road, bear right in 100m, and pass **Bembridge Windmill**. Stay in your current direction and turn left on reaching the road (in effect, straight on). Look out for and follow BB3 on your left (450m). Bear right with the main path after 250m. ◄ Ignore ways off and emerge onto the harbour road. A detour into Beach Road opposite will reward with a 180° sea view at **Bembridge Point** (limited accommodation, supermarket, pubs, cafés, restaurants, shops, toilets).

Alternatively, it is possible to detour back into Brading Marshes for a while (you will need to return the same way).

To return to Seaview, continue around **Bembridge Harbour**, passing bus stops. Cross the Eastern Yar (1.3km) and take the first right (Latimer Road). Keep to this direction until following the sea wall, which becomes a delightful causeway above the marshland. It is possible you will have just the seabirds for company!

At the end of the causeway bear half-left on a faint path through **St Helens Duver** and aim for the pillared Old Club House to the left – now a National Trust holiday cottage. At the junction a little further on, take R85 (opposite) through two fields, linked by a footbridge over a stream (bear left just after it). At the far left corner of the second field turn right onto a lane and shortly bear left into the drive of the **Priory Bay Hotel**. A footpath shortly branches away from the drive, and in only 250m swing right with the main path to retrace the walk's initial section down to **Seagrove Bay** and the short seaside stroll back to **Seaview**.

WALK 29
Wootton Bridge circular

Start/Finish	Wootton Bridge, opposite the Sloop Inn
Distance	15.9km (10 miles)
Grade	Fairly easy
Time	5½hrs
Refreshments	Havenstreet (11.5km), Fishbourne (14.8km)
Public transport	Bus routes 4 and 9
Parking	Opposite the Sloop Inn (customers only). The car park in Brannon Way is short stay. New Road may have possibilities.
Early finish	Near Havenstreet station (3.5km, bus route 34), Havenstreet (11.7km, bus route 34), or near Quarr Abbey (13.5km, bus routes 4 and 9). Route 34 runs weekdays only; the last service is about 2pm.

This consistently delightful walk is replete with trees, so do it when they are in full leaf! It dips into three of the numerous ancient woods surrounding the village of Havenstreet and features the seductive sight and sound of steam trains on the Isle of Wight Steam Railway. It might be a good idea, then, to do this walk when the railway is running: the route twice crosses the line, and in summer you won't have to wait long to see the trains. Note that this walk is not possible during the annual 'Bestival' music festival in early September.

From **Wootton Bridge** (supermarket, pubs, restaurants, shops, toilets) take bridleway N1 heading south, with the lake (Old Mill Pond) on the left. In 80m branch right, bear left almost immediately, and in 350m cross a stile on the left to enter Hurst Copse. At the end of a boardwalk, bear

On days when the trains are running frequently it's well worth waiting here until you see one – quite an experience!

left for a short detour to a secluded part of the lake, then return to continue along the other fork, which leads back to the original track, now opposite a former ice house. Turn left to walk along this pleasant bridleway, eventually crossing the steam railway line for the first time. ◄

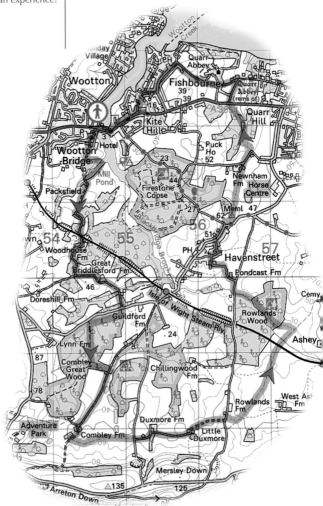

Continue on a stony track to a T-junction and turn left (N15). Having walked round **Great Briddlesford Farm** go through a metal gate to continue on a path between hedgerows. Emerge onto a road beside bus stops, then turn right and almost immediately left on an inconspicuous path now inside **Combley Great Wood**, which is over 50 per cent oak. Turn right at a junction of paths beside a group of conifers (150m), heading deeper into the wood on a rough, potentially boggy track. Then at a T-junction turn right and almost immediately sharp left to continue to another T-junction. Take the minor track left to a T-junction outside the wood and turn right. ▶

Bear left through **Combley Farm** (800m) and in a further 200m, just before a cattle grid, turn sharp left through one field and left again inside a second. Continue through two more fields and keep to your current direction on a track. At a junction after 200m swing right – following the yellow arrow – shortly ignoring **Duxmore Farm** on your left to ascend in your current direction. At a junction of paths by a house continue uphill on a stony track, eventually reaching a lane. Turn left and immediately right, with a grand view ahead towards Ashey sea mark.

Aim for a fence to the left of the copse ahead and go through the gate to enter another field. Bear half-left, still with no path, never straying far from the left field edge. Go through another gate in the far side of the field and continue in your current direction – a lovely rural scene. Keep the field boundary on the left – including long gaps in the hedgerow – and recross the stream railway line to pick up a faint grassy path. In 350m turn left on R19 and soon enter the enchanting, mostly coniferous Kemphill Moor Copse.

Ignore the initial right turn and keep to the main path, eventually leaving the wood and continuing to a lane to take a right turn. Take the first lane on the left and turn right at a T-junction, now in the village of **Havenstreet** (pub). ▶ Turn right at a second T-junction and, at the junction with Firestone Copse Road by a bus stop, cross the stile ahead and ascend the hillock towards a large brick First World War **memorial** at the top.

The fields soon passed on the left host 'Bestival', the nationally famous music festival.

For the pub turn left at this junction.

Kemphill Moor Copse

Cross to the next field, with the mainland now in view, and continue in the same direction through more fields to pass to the right of **Newnham Farm** and onto a lane. Still keeping to your current direction, bear left in 70m through a gate and continue diagonally across the field towards another gate, just visible. Cross it to continue beside a lake. On reaching the main road just east of **Fishbourne** turn left to find the bus stops or, to continue back to **Wootton Bridge** (2.4km), cross the road to follow R4a and turn left on the Coastal Path by the Quarr Abbey ruins (see Walk 3 for details).

WALK 30

Wootton Bridge to Newport

Start	Wootton Bridge, opposite the Sloop Inn
Finish	Newport bus station
Distance	9.4km (5.9 miles)
Grade	Easy
Time	3hrs
Refreshments	Wootton (1.7km), Island Harbour Marina (5.8km)
Public transport	*From start* Bus routes 4 and 9; *from finish* Bus routes 1, 2, 3, 5, 6, 7, 8, 9 and 12
Parking	Opposite the Sloop Inn (customers only). The car park in Brannon Way is short stay. New Road may have possibilities.
Early finish	Wootton (1.9km, bus route 9), A3054 (5.2km, bus route 9)

Strolling along the western bank of the Medina estuary is a very worthwhile experience, and the initial woodland section of this walk adds variety. There are three stages: the first gradually heads towards the Medina from Wootton Bridge by crossing the steam railway heritage line near Wootton station and continuing on the line's former course, before starting a circuit of Fattingpark Copse and reaching Island Harbour Marina midway along the estuary; the second is the ramble beside the estuary itself into Newport; and the third is Newport itself, notably two of its most interesting streets (Quay Street and Watchbell Lane) and some of its notable buildings (particularly the Guildhall).

From **Wootton Bridge** (supermarket, pubs, restaurants, shops, toilets) take bridleway N1 heading south, with the lake (Old Mill Pond) on your left. In 80m branch right, then in 50m bear right again into Fernhill Park, either along the drive and cycle track or through the wood to the right (which eventually joins the track). Emerge at and continue along a residential street to a more major road. Turn left, then almost immediately left again into Packsfield Lane, which soon becomes an

Trains used to run
along here from
Ryde to Cowes
via Newport, and
this stretch – from
Wootton to Newport
– is considered the
most likely candidate
on the former
railway network for
restoration.

attractive wide path. Look out for **Wootton station** – a
steam railway terminus – on your right.

Cross the railway line and turn right (N6) to ascend to
a road at **Wootton Common** and here turn left, immediately passing the Woodmans Arms pub. Turn right at the
roundabout (or continue ahead for bus stops) and right
again just after 'Quarrels Copse' in 150m along a grassy
path between gardens. Continue through a wood, ignoring path offshoots. On reaching a T-junction, turn left on
the disused railway track, which is an extension of the
current preserved steam railway crossed earlier. ◄

Cross a road to continue on the old railway
track. At a track crossroads (500m) turn left into

190

Fattingpark Copse. ▶ Where the main track swings right (200m), continue in your current direction. In a further 200m swing right with the main path along the edge of the wood, at the end of which turn right (N115), shortly with the first splendid view of the Medina.

Continuing along the track would be the most direct route, but this circuitous option adds a bit more diversity.

> The **River Medina** estuary ('Medina' is a corruption of the Saxon *medene*, meaning 'middle river'), which runs from Newport to Cowes, is so prominent, especially when viewed on the map, that most people probably don't realise that the 17km-long river actually rises from the north face of St Catherine's Down, some distance to the south of Newport. As with all island rivers, the estuary mudflats and saltmarsh attract a wide variety of birds, both resident (such as mallards, mute swans, coot) and over-wintering (such as Brent geese, widgeon, teal). In the 18th and 19th centuries the estuary provided a resting place for vessels transporting convicts to Australia.

At a T-junction with a track turn left to go under the railway track (the same one as before) to reach a main road. ▶ Cross here to continue along N121, which arrives at **Island Harbour Marina**.

The nearest bus stops are some way along on the left.

Beside the Medina

The East Medina tidal mill was built at **Island Harbour Marina** in 1790 and was used until 1939, additionally serving as barracks during the early 1800s to house friendly foreign soldiers and French PoWs after the Napoleonic Wars. The building was demolished in 1950 after a major fire, to be replaced by the marina in the mid-1960s. Look out for Tide Mill House on the right just before the marina: it was built for the original mill owner in 1790.

Continue to the river bank and turn left to start the riverside meander towards Newport. The once-esteemed 1930s paddle-steamer *Ryde Queen* has been lying derelict here for decades now, scandalously rusting away. In 1.7km notice the trees of Newport Arboretum to the left. Soon after passing a hotel and restaurant, you emerge on a drive at the start of Newport Quay.

Continue along the quay and walk under the road bridge. This is now the start of the estuary, fed by the Medina flowing in from the left, and another tributary – Lukely Brook – from the right. Pass the Grade II listed Dolphin Inn to continue up Quay Street.

Looking towards Newport

Quay Street is arguably the most elegant and evocative street in Newport, full of 17th- and 18th-century town houses and small, charming hotels. It was constructed as part of Richard de Redvers' original 12th-century town layout and would have been the 'entrance to the town' for those arriving by boat.

At the top of Quay Street is the neoclassical Grade II listed Guildhall: built by John Nash and finished in 1816, it hosts the very informative **Island History Museum**. Turn right down quaint Watchbell Lane, turn sharp left at the end of the short parade, and go straight across the crossroads, keeping the minster on your right. Carry on across another crossroads to come to a major junction. Newport bus station is on your right.

WALK 31
Bembridge Trail

Start	Newport bus station
Finish	Bembridge Point
Distance	19.8km (12.4 miles)
Grade	Fairly easy after a moderate ascent
Time	6½hrs
Refreshments	Arreton (5.4km), Brading (14.7km)
Public transport	*To start* Bus routes 1, 2, 3, 5, 6, 7, 8, 9 and 12; *from finish* Bus route 8
Parking	The nearest long-stay car park is 5mins' walk away – at Coppins Bridge, near the multiplex
Early finish	Arreton (5.3km, bus route 8 and seasonal Downs Breezer), Knighton (8.8km, Downs Breezer), Brading (14.7km, bus routes 2 and 3)

The Bembridge Trail is one of the island's official trails and well worth walking in its entirety. Meandering across the east of the island from capital to coast, it follows and shadows the downland stretching roughly between Newport and Brading – sometimes on the ridge, sometimes in the valley – and there is always something attractive in sight to maintain interest. The Brading to Bembridge section resembles something of a coda: quite different to what has gone before, it initially traverses Brading Marshes – the only RSPB nature reserve on the island – before ascending to the National Trust's Bembridge Windmill and the final stretch to Bembridge Point. A short and pleasant prelude beside the Medina is included to enable a start from central Newport.

From **Newport** bus station head east along South Street and take the third right (Furrlongs), turning right again on footpath N218 (70m). Keep the River Medina on the right, in 700m crossing it and turning left to reach a road. Cross the adjacent main road and take St Georges Lane ahead, following a signpost for byway A28 and ascending **St George's Down** – now at the official start of the Bembridge Trail.

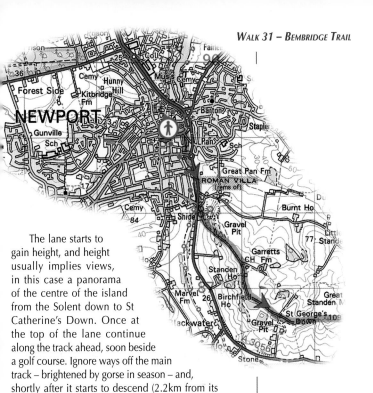

The lane starts to gain height, and height usually implies views, in this case a panorama of the centre of the island from the Solent down to St Catherine's Down. Once at the top of the lane continue along the track ahead, soon beside a golf course. Ignore ways off the main track – brightened by gorse in season – and, shortly after it starts to descend (2.2km from its start), at a two-armed signpost topped by a 'Great East Standen' sign turn left and immediately right over a stile – a minor but very worthwhile deviation from the official trail on account of the view.

Map continues on page 196

Spot the village down below (Arreton), and descend the pathless grass towards it. Find a gap in the bracken leading to a stile and descend the edge of a field (sweet-smelling rapeseed in May) towards a road. At the nearby junction turn left onto the main road in **Arreton** (pub; Arreton Old Village also has a pub and shops). Pass bus stops, and just past the White Lion pub there is the option to detour left to explore **Arreton Old Village** (see Walk 33).

Turn left into School Lane 110m past the pub. Take either parallel fork in 90m, but when they converge keep to the left of the hedge. At a track T-junction turn right

195

and immediately left beside an artificial lake, still in the shadow of the downs to the north. Notice the church of Newchurch on the hillside to the southeast. Ignore ways off until a five-way path junction (800m). Take either of the parallel tracks ahead – both ascend to a lane where the walk turns left. Turn right on NC1 (70m) and swing right with the track.

At a road turn left, soon passing bus stops. This is Knighton, located in a beautiful and very green little pocket of the island – a riot of colour in the autumn. Turn right 200m from the bus stops (NC45). In a further 400m, with Harts Ash Farm visible ahead, turn right on a wide track with overhanging branches. Ignore ways off this lovely track; then, in 1km with another farm in view, take the track sharp right initially away from it. In 80m turn left (B33a), and once on the other side of the farm stay on the main track, continuing to ascend the down. Soon Shanklin and Sandown Bay come into view. Cross the road at the top of the down and turn right, soon with a wonderful view towards Nettlestone and St Helens and, later, Ryde and Portsmouth.

Turn left on B26 (600m), and at the foot of the descent turn left through a metal gate to follow the grassy path ahead. Keep to the main path, which eventually descends to **Nunwell Farm**. At a T-junction just past the farm turn left, and in 150m go right (B23) over the pathless grass following the direction indicated by the signpost. Towards the top of a giant second field head towards a

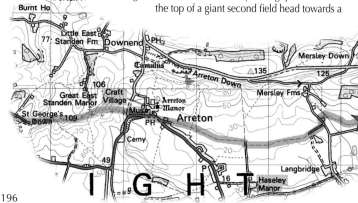

fence just visible ahead, soon noticing **Nunwell House** to the right, in the shadow of Brading Down.

> A beautiful house set in equally beautiful gardens, **Nunwell House** was the Oglander family's residence from 1522 until 1980, and it was here that King Charles I spent his last night before being imprisoned in Carisbrooke. The house is worth an afternoon's outing, but opening hours are limited.

Pass to the right of the farm which the field encloses, the village of Brading – your destination – soon visible. Continue through a third field, heading towards a solitary house. On reaching a road turn right with care, passing the entrance to Nunwell House and bearing right into Doctors Lane a little further ahead. At a tarmac junction inside the village, bear left down Cross Street to reach the centre of **Brading** (pubs, fish and chip shop, grocery store, toilets), next to the Lilliput Antique Doll and Toy Museum.

Turn right for the pubs and village store, otherwise left. Turn into Quay Lane, just before the church, to pass Old Rectory Mansion, reputedly the oldest house on

Map continues on page 200

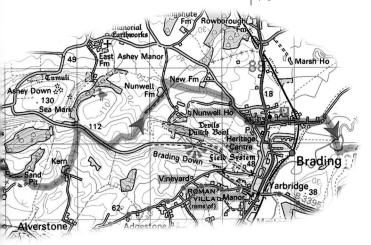

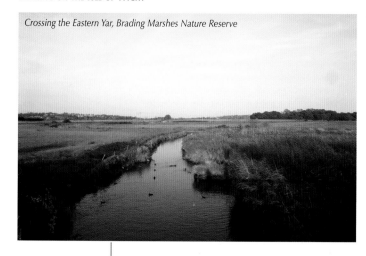

Crossing the Eastern Yar, Brading Marshes Nature Reserve

Alternatively, to end the walk here continue past the church to reach bus stops.

the island. ◄ Cross the railway line and in 250m keep straight on (B3), now in **Brading Marshes Nature Reserve**. In 150m bear left with the obvious path, soon crossing one branch of the Eastern Yar and then another. Be sure to bear left at the junction just after this second branch. Continue through this very lovely belt of woodland, with a lagoon on the right.

Brading Marshes Nature Reserve was originally an extension of today's Bembridge Harbour. The enlarged area was known as Brading Harbour or Brading Haven. It was only in 1878 that the building of an embankment from Bembridge to St Helens 'turned sea into land'. It is the island's sole RSPB reserve, although by no means its sole bird magnet (other popular spots include Newtown Harbour). Ironically, man's drainage methods have arguably become too successful, and the RSPB are working to retain a distinct wetland environment for the benefit of wading birds and their admirers. Birds that might be seen include buzzards, warblers and lapwings (spring), woodpeckers and wagtails (summer), swallows and housemartins (autumn), and widgeon and yellowhammer (winter). Buzzards and owls may also be spotted. The small areas of woodland in the centre of reserve, such as Centurion's Copse, are termed 'ancient' (in existence before 1600) and provide a haven for red squirrels as well as playing host to daffodils, primroses, celandines, violets and bluebells.

At the next path junction, by a 'Centurion's Copse' sign, bear left again. Turn left at the T-junction ahead, staying just within woodland, and soon emerge back into the open. Keep to the main path, with the Lord Yarborough Monument soon visible on the right and the village of St Helens on the left. On crossing into a second field, Bembridge Windmill becomes visible on the rise ahead – the path keeps heading towards it. Bembridge Airport is also nearby.

It may take a bit longer than expected to reach Bembridge Windmill – but reach it you will. Turn left at the T-junction beside the entrance, and turn left on reaching the road (in effect straight on).

Bembridge Windmill

Bembridge Windmill was in operation between 1700 and 1913 and is the last remaining windmill on the island, still containing much of its original machinery. Turner painted it during his visit to the island in 1795. One of many 1960s island acquisitions by the National Trust, it may be visited between mid-March and early November.

At this point it is possible to detour back into Brading Marshes for a while (but return here to continue the route).

Look out for and follow BB3 on your left (450m), then bear right with the main path after 250m. ◀ Ignore ways off and emerge onto the harbour road. Turn left for the bus stops, perhaps enjoying refreshments at the pub or café while waiting, or turn up Beach Road for a wonderful sea view at **Bembridge Point** (limited accommodation, supermarket, pubs, cafés, restaurants, shops, toilets).

WALK 32
Worsley Trail

Start	Three Bishops pub, Brighstone
Finish	Shanklin Old Village
Distance	20km (12.5 miles)
Grade	Moderate (occasionally strenuous)
Time	7hrs
Refreshments	Shorwell (4.6km), Godshill (12.8km), Wroxall (16.5km)
Public transport	*To start* Bus route 12; *from finish* Bus routes 2 and 3, and train
Parking	Warnes Lane car park (behind the Three Bishops pub)
Early finish	Shorwell (4.3km, bus route 12), near Chillerton (6.7km, bus route 6), Godshill (12.8km, bus routes 2 and 3), Wroxall (16.1km, bus route 3)
Note	The official starting point of the trail, at the National Trust car park on the Brighstone–Calbourne road, has no direct access by bus, and the initial section duplicates the Tennyson Trail, so an alternative start from Brighstone has been chosen and is, in fact, one of the highlights of the walk.

The Worsley Trail provides a link between the downland of the Back of the Wight and the southeast downland – the only walk in this book to do so. There is also the bold, glorious descent into Shanklin, preceded by some incredible views of Sandown Bay and the island's third major chain of downs radiating east from Newport to Bembridge. In between is pleasant, if unexceptional countryside, with pockets of interest such as remote New Barn Farm beneath the majesty of the Chillerton Down transmitter.

From the Three Bishops in **Brighstone** (limited accommodation, pub, restaurant/café, food shops, toilets), walk towards the newsagents and turn right up North Street, one of the island's most unashamedly olde-worlde streets with its cute post office, National Trust shop and small museum. At the T-junction turn right and, on meeting your original road, left on footpath BS30 (200m). Almost immediately an impressive view opens up behind, and

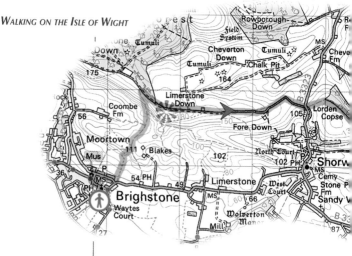

the path soon starts to ascend the downland ahead. At the top, continue on BS80 heading for the bulk that is Limerstone Down. Ignore ways off and eventually swing left to ascend the down – a tough climb.

Topograph atop Limerstone Down

On reaching the ridge turn right. When the forest ends and a northerly view opens up, stay on the ridge, shortly reaching the **Limerstone Down** viewpoint (just off route), which you may share with a herd of cows.

Map continues on
page 204

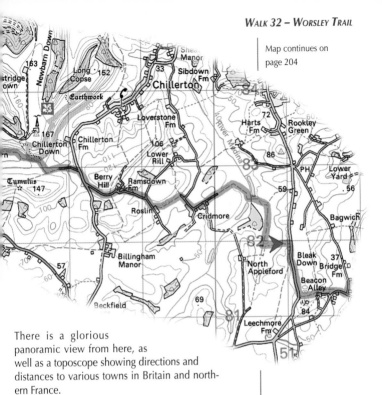

There is a glorious
panoramic view from here, as
well as a toposcope showing directions and
distances to various towns in Britain and northern France.

Continue along the ridge and stay on the track to
reach a road. Cross this and take SW49 opposite. ▶ Walk
around two sides of a vast field before going through a
gate and swinging left with the track. On meeting another
track turn sharp right towards isolated **New Barn Farm**
in the valley. Just before the farm gate, turn left over the
pathless grass, soon passing a signpost and ascending
very steeply. Continue around the base of Northcourt
Down and **Chillerton Down**, always ignoring ways off
the salient grassy path, now in remotest countryside
below the 230m (755ft) transmitter.

Eventually a road is reached. Turn right, then left by
bus stops at the top of the hill, and right at a T-junction
some distance ahead. Turn left on G14 (150m), pass

Alternatively, turn
right for a 10–20mins
return detour into
Shorwell, where there
is a pub, shop and
bus stops.

Ramsdown Farm, and on reaching a lane continue in the same direction, with **Cridmore Farm** on the right. Soon swing left with the lane, and at the end of the farm buildings continue in the same direction. After crossing one field and entering a second, immediately turn right with the path, soon walking through a short wooded section.

Keep a hedgerow on your left, meet a track in 650m, and in a further 100m turn left by a signpost. Once at the road turn right, and after 50m take the parallel path. Eventually come onto the road again and cross to the right to take GL15. Immediately bear left off the track to continue through a wooden gate, soon with a near panoramic view encompassing (clockwise) Arreton Down, Bembridge Down, Stenbury Down and St Catherine's Down. Notice also the tower of Godshill Church straight ahead.

Descend to a gate and continue towards Godshill. Keep to the far right of this field and the next, and descend to a lane. Turn left and soon left again (Bagwich Lane), in 150m turning right on GL21. Fork right in 200m, shortly crossing the Eastern Yar in woodland and abruptly arriving at and skirting round a delightful pond inhabited by

Map continues on page 206

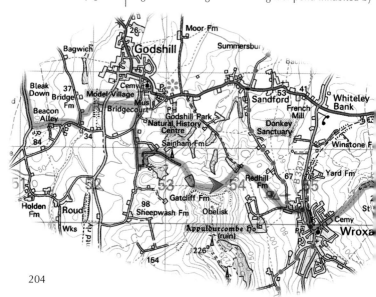

Freemantle Gate

(at the time of writing at least) some particularly noisy ducks! Cross a road to continue ahead, and at the next lane turn right. ▶

Shortly after a lane comes in from the left, turn left on Sheepwash Lane and in 400m left again on GL56. Ignore the descending path by **Sainham Farm**, soon go through a large metal gate and ascend towards trees. At a major path junction (350m) bear left uphill between a wire fence and a hedge, soon with a comprehensive view north to north-east and a stone wall on your right, once the boundary wall of the Appuldurcombe estate. Descend to and walk through neoclassical Freemantle Gate (see Walk 20), and after just 70m branch off the track towards the village of Wroxall below, ignoring ways off.

Time and energy permitting, however, it is worth making the 15mins return detour to **Appuldurcombe House** further along the ridge.

Baroque **Appuldurcombe House**, once the grandest house on the island and with grounds landscaped by 'Capability' Brown, was built for the noble and

Alternatively, go left for a few hundred metres to detour into the popular, photogenic village of Godshill (pubs, cafés, shops, toilets) for refreshments and bus stops.

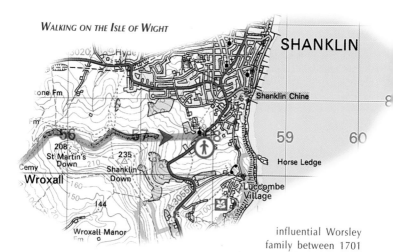

influential Worsley family between 1701 and 1770. A 12th-century priory once stood on the site, so it is perhaps apt that the house was used by a Benedictine order about a century ago before a permanent home was found for them at Quarr Abbey. Now owned by English Heritage, the house contains a permanent exhibition of house-related photographs, although sadly the interior itself is in ruins following a Second World War bombing raid. Next to the house is an owl and falconry centre.

Emerging on a drive turn left, soon reaching the main road through **Wroxall** (grocery store, pubs) beside bus stops.

> **Wroxall** is idyllically situated in a valley with the southeast downs on three sides, and consequently in the centre of prime walking country. It was a relatively remote agricultural village before the advent of the railway in 1866, at which time the village was extended to accommodate the railway workers. The parish church was built some 10 years later with stone bored from the railway tunnel to Ventnor.

Ascend the rightmost of the two sets of steps across the road and turn right on the disused Shanklin–Ventnor railway line at the top to reach a bridge close to the village church and pub. Wroxall station used to be just across the road, but today there is no trace of it. Cross the bridge and bear left up Castle Road, branching right on V30 just beyond Wroxall cemetery. In 450m ignore paths to the left and right, now on the lower slopes of **St Martin's Down**, and in a further 200m pass a memorial stone for Cook's Castle.

> **Cook's Castle** was nothing more than an 18th-century folly erected by Capability Brown as part of his commission by Sir Richard Worsley to improve the Appuldurcombe estate. It was demolished in the middle of the 20th century.

Stray into a wood, still ignoring ways off, and having exited back onto the open down bear half-left following a just-discernable path, with a truly sensational view opening up of Sandown Bay and the entire ridge of downland from Culver Down in the east to St George's Down in the west (and beyond, almost as far as Newport). In about 70m bear left towards the trees, again on the faintest of paths, and beyond a gate keep the steep incline just to the left. Eventually you start the grand descent towards Shanklin: a cracking finish! Emerge in the delightful churchyard of the Old Parish Church and turn left on the road for the short walk into **Shanklin** (supermarket, pubs, cafés, restaurants, shops, toilets). The bus stops (route 3) are 200m away, just before the Old Village.

WALK 33

Shorwell to Brading

Start	Crown Inn, Shorwell
Finish	Brading
Distance	20.4km (12.8 miles)
Grade	Moderate to strenuous
Time	7½hrs
Refreshments	Arreton (11.1km)
Public transport	*To start* Bus route 12; *from finish* Bus routes 2 and 3, and train
Parking	Crown Inn car park (customers only)
Early finish	Near Chillerton (2.6km, bus route 6), Rookley (6.2km, bus route 3), Merstone (9.2km, bus route 2), Arreton (10.9km, bus route 8 and seasonal Downs Breezer), Knighton (15.4km, seasonal Downs Breezer)

This long walk traverses two under-explored stretches of downland: to the east of Shorwell and the east of Arreton. Both villages have much to offer the visitor too: Shorwell its thatched cottages and woodland setting, and Arreton its touristy but tasteful 'old village' and church with Saxon features. There are ample opportunities to shorten the walk, but plenty of stunning views make it well worth staying to the end. Choose a day when a southwesterly is blowing to help drive you along!

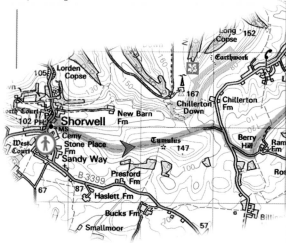

From the Crown Inn in **Shorwell** (limited accommodation, pub, shop), head east past the church and village store. Immediately beyond the latter, turn right onto footpath SW13. The path rises almost immediately, with Shorwell seen nestling below the trees and a marvellous, increasingly panoramic view opening up. At a junction in 1.5km bear left with the main path. Descend to a track and here turn right, briefly following the Worsley Trail. Descend further to a road, turn right, and on the brow of a hill, by bus stops, turn left up a lane. In 350m turn left (G15) to climb back on a ridge.

Map continues on page 212

Take a quick look around: the Back of the Wight coastline is to the west, Bembridge Down to the

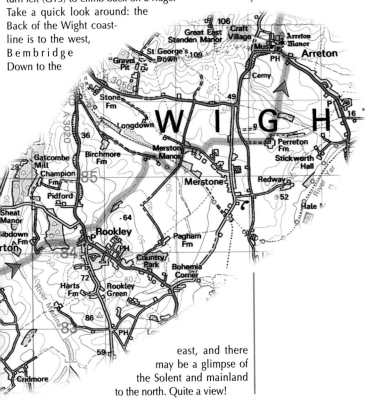

east, and there may be a glimpse of the Solent and mainland to the north. Quite a view!

Turn right and at a junction of paths continue on G15, still on the ridge. In 400m ignore a gate on the right, but in a further 500m, by a telegraph pole, bear right to descend through a field. Turn right on the lane and, in 100m, left on G19. Keep to your current direction – and cross an infant **River Medina** – until, in the middle of a field after 550m, the path swings left to cross a stile into woodland. Turn right to continue on this very attractive track, eventually emerging in the village of **Rookley**, once an important brick-making and gravel-quarrying centre. ◄

Bus stops are 100m to the right.

To continue, turn left on the road and in 90m right on A37 with views towards Arreton Down – where you'll be soon. At a T-junction in 1.3km turn right (briefly sharing the way with the Stenbury Trail), and go left at the next junction (450m), soon crossing the disused Newport–Sandown railway line. At a crossroads by a beautiful early 17th-century house (**Merston Manor**) turn right, and in 250m left on A1. Cross a drive and continue through three fields to a road and bus stops, the scenery slowly improving.

Cross the road and, shortly, a parallel lane to continue on a stony track. At **Perreton Farm** turn left through three gates; shortly after the third, turn sharp left up an escarpment to cross a stile. At a T-junction turn right, then, in 40m, go left downhill before steeply ascending the next escarpment through the gorse (no path) and over another stile. Continue towards the spread-out village of Arreton and the downland ridge of the walk's next stage.

Turn left at the road through **Arreton** (pub; Arreton Old Village also has a pub and shops), close to bus stops. Then at the White Lion pub turn right up A12, but then immediately left to enter the 'Roman Garden' of the lavender and lace shop and so start a semi-circuit of so-called Arreton Old Village: a hotch-potch of olde-worlde shops and eateries, aimed squarely at tourists but no less charming for that. Arrive at a T-junction facing the church and turn left to ascend **Arreton Down**, soon with a good view back towards the church and the southeast downs beyond.

Arreton Church

Church of St. George
• ARRETON •
FOUNDED PRIOR TO THE NORMAN CONQUEST.
ENLARGED IN THE 12ᵀᴴ AND 13ᵀᴴ CENTURIES.
IN THE CHURCHYARD IS THE GRAVE OF
ELIZABETH WALLBRIDGE, LEGH RICHMONDS
"DAIRYMAN'S DAUGHTER".

Arreton Church was reconstructed in the 12th century (with later additions), but remains of the original Saxon church can still be seen, such as the faded wall-painting and narrow window in the north wall, and the middle window in the west wall.

Bear right past an information board towards the top of the down, and continue along its ridge admiring the spectacular 180° view (the best yet) and the wonderful, bracing air.

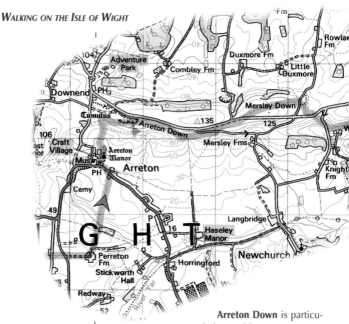

Arreton Down is particularly noted for its Great Green Bush Cricket population, but also hosts a wide variety of birds (such as kestrel, buzzard and woodpecker) and flowers (up to 40 species per square metre, including vetches, scabious and harebells). Winter grazing keeps the less graceful vegetation at bay.

Head towards a gate in the distance, shortly after power cables. Having crossed it, continue on a narrow path, still at the top of the ridge. Stay near the top until a hollow blocks the way; find and follow the path leading in and around it to reach a wooden barrier, which is crossed to emerge on a country lane. Turn left and in 70m sharp right on A16, almost immediately turning left to ascend to a path T-junction just shy of the main road. Turn right.

Just after the field on your right ends, go through a gap in the hedgerow to cross the road and continue quarter-right on R16, over the pathless grass towards the top of

Mersley Down, now with
an additional view north incorpo-
rating several belts of woodland, Havenstreet, Ryde and
the South Downs of the mainland. Post holes recently discovered on the down's southern slope (beyond the road)
are evidence of an iron-age vineyard. The panoramic view
at the top is one of the best on the island.

Descend in the same direction, half-left from the
road, and in a few hundred metres head towards a footpath signpost, increasingly visible. Turn right on the lane
and in 80m take R17 half-right across the pathless grass
towards a soon-visible signpost. Cross the road to continue on NC2. Immediately bear right over a stile and,
after admiring the expanse of woodland below, continue
towards the wood straight ahead on a faint path, aiming for a stile visible below, just north of the hamlet of
Knighton. ▶ Find and follow bridleway NC4 nearly
opposite – a curiously atmospheric valley path – eventually ascending steeply to a T-junction. Here turn left, and
left again on a narrow path just before a road.

In 80m cross the road and ascend the field, quarter-
left, to the sea mark on top of **Ashey Down** and another
exquisite view, this time incorporating Nettlestone,
St Helens and Bembridge.

There is a bus stop
150m on the right.

The **sea mark** was erected in 1735 to convey sema-phore signals to Portsmouth in respect of maritime craft in the island's waters. It can be seen when crossing the Solent from Portsmouth, and can be reached from Ryde on foot by heading up Union Street from the Esplanade and carrying on for some considerable distance!

With your back to the sea mark, head towards the bushes ahead, half-left from the road. In about 200m follow a faint path coming in from the left, heading obliquely towards a belt of woodland in the valley below. Always keep to the rightmost fork while descending (where practicable), eventually reaching the valley floor in a beautiful location. Continue past two troughs to find a stile tucked away on the right. Follow B34 and, at the next junction, turn left on B24. In 300m bear left to enter another copse, then immediately bear right.

Once back in the open, cross a stile to walk through a vast field. Stay in your current direction through three more fields, occupied by distinguished oak trees and pos-sibly curious cows. Towards the top of the giant fourth field, head towards a fence just visible ahead, soon noticing Nunwell House to the right, in the shadow of **Brading Down** (see Walk 31). Pass to the right of the farm that the field encloses, with the village of Brading – your destination – soon visible. Yet another lovely setting.

Continue through a fifth and final field heading towards a solitary house. On reaching a road turn right with care, passing the entrance to **Nunwell House** and bearing right into Doctors Lane a little further ahead. At the tarmac junction inside **Brading** (pubs, fish and chip shop, grocery store, toilets), continue down West Street to reach the Town Hall and the bus stops. For Brading station, follow the road around the bend and take Station Road on the left.

WALK 34
Godshill to Ventnor

Start	The Griffin pub, Godshill
Finish	Ventnor
Distance	7.4km (4.6 miles)
Grade	Moderate
Time	3hrs
Refreshments	None en route
Public transport	*To start* Bus routes 2 and 3; *from finish* Bus routes 3 and 6
Parking	Car park opposite The Griffin pub
Early finish	Wroxall (5.1km, bus route 3)

This is a particularly beautiful downland walk, perfect for a sunny day. A little-used permissive path starting just south of Godshill ascends to the transmitter on top of Appuldurcombe Down, which provides a sensational view. After following the ridge of Stenbury Down and descending to the Wroxall valley, there is a steep ascent of Wroxall Down, with a tranquil sea opening up around. A magnificent view of Ventnor from up on high is one of the highlights of the walk.

Walk up Hollow Lane next to The Griffin in **Godshill** (pubs, cafés, shops, toilets), turning left almost immediately onto footpath GL57. After entering woodland bear right at the fork immediately ahead. Turn right at a T-junction, now out of the wood, and left at another a short distance later. Soon go through a large metal gate to ascend towards trees. At a major path junction (350m) the first path on the right (GL49) is the Stenbury Trail, but instead take the rightmost of the two paths ahead and immediately turn right over the stile onto a permissive footpath.

Be sure to take the rightmost of two gates in 250m, after which the path is less enclosed and a southwesterly vista opens up. In a further 200m, at an inconspicuous junction of faint paths, bear left away from a stone

WALKING ON THE ISLE OF WIGHT

wall towards a gate. Swing right with the path and bear left uphill immediately on entering the next field, keeping gorse bushes on your left. Then at the end of the bushes at the top of the current incline bear right on a wide, grassy path, ascending gradually, with the view ever more comprehensive. Go through a gate (350m) and bear left towards the radio transmitter on top of **Appuldurcombe Down** for an incredible panoramic view. Look to the southeast to spot Whitwell, and Niton beyond.

Head along the concrete track leading from the transmitter to pass a second transmitter further along the ridge, now on **Stenbury Down**. Spot the Ventnor suburb of Lowtherville ahead to your left. Ignore all descents from the ridge; but, in 900m, look out for and cross a stile on the left which descends initially through a golf course. Follow the yellow arrows and in 350m cross a more obvious path to descend towards – but not through – fieldgates, remaining on a faint path. Having descended to a lane running through the valley, turn left and follow the stone wall to continue on V13, which ascends

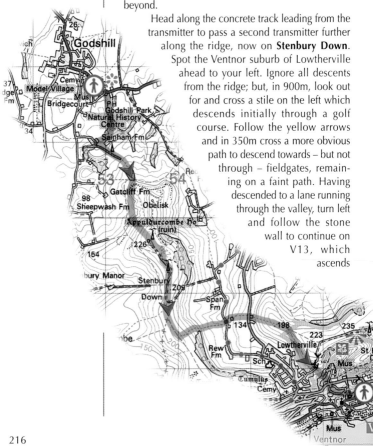

to the main road and bus stops. Cross to continue on the footpath opposite, ignoring ways off. The sea soon becomes visible – a picture of serenity.

On top of Stenbury Down, looking east over Wroxall

The path leads onto Wroxall Down, now with panoramic views. But the best is yet to come! Bear right off the main path just beyond a bench and signpost, initially in the direction of the sea. Ignore path offshoots. On reaching a lane on the left (440m) bear half-right on an indistinct path, shortly spotting and crossing a stile on the left leading onto the lane. Turn left and immediately right to find one of the most magnificent views on this side of the island: Ventnor spread out at your feet, with miles of sea to the southeast beyond.

Descend the very steep path, staying near the fence when it peters out. Descend steps and turn right at the bottom to reach a road and bus stops. ▸ To reach the centre of **Ventnor** (accommodation, supermarket, pubs, cafés, restaurants, shops, toilets), take the sloping path opposite and first right (Tulse Hill) to emerge at the bus stop in Ventnor High Street.

You may wish to detour into the adjacent industrial estate, formerly Ventnor station. Steam trains from Ryde used to use the tunnel still visible at the far end.

217

APPENDIX A

Route summary table

COASTAL PATH (NORTH COAST)

Walk no.	Walk title	Distance	Time	Grade	Refreshments en route?	Early finish option?	Page
1	Sandown to Bembridge Point	9.8km (6.1 miles)	3½hrs	Moderate	Yes	Yes	39
2	Bembridge Point to Ryde	9.3km (5.8 miles)	3hrs	Moderate	Yes	Yes	44
3	Ryde to Cowes	12.1km (7.6 miles)	4hrs	Fairly easy	Yes	Yes	50
4	Cowes to Yarmouth	24km (15 miles)	9hrs	Easy	Yes	Yes	56
5	Yarmouth to Alum Bay	9.1km (5.7 miles)	3hrs	Moderate	Yes	Yes	64

COASTAL PATH (SOUTH COAST)

Walk no.	Walk title	Distance	Time	Grade	Refreshments en route?	Early finish option?	Page
6	Sandown to Ventnor	9.2km (5.8 miles)	3½hrs	Easy–moderate	Yes	Yes	69
7	Ventnor to Chale	10km (6.3 miles)	4hrs	Moderate	Yes	Yes	74
8	Chale to Brook	12.7km (7.9 miles)	4hrs	Mainly easy	Yes	Limited	79
9	Brook to Alum Bay	10.3km (6.5 miles)	4hrs	Moderate	Yes	Yes	84

WEST WIGHT

Walk no.	Walk title	Distance	Time	Grade	Refreshments en route?	Early finish option?	Page
10	Shorwell circular	14km (8.8 miles)	5hrs	Moderate	No	Limited	90
11	Shorwell to Niton	12.4km (7.7 miles)	4hrs	Fairly easy–moderate	No	Yes	94
12	Brighstone circular	11.4km (7.1 miles)	3½hrs	Moderate	Yes*	Limited	100
13	Brighstone to Yarmouth	11.3km (7.1 miles)	3½hrs	Moderate	No	Yes	104
14	Best of eastern Freshwater (circular)	9.8km (6.1 miles)	3hrs	Easy	Yes	Yes	109
15	Best of western Freshwater (circular)	13.9km (8.7 miles)	5hrs	Moderate	Yes	Yes	114

16	Shalfleet and Newtown circular	10.2km (6.4 miles)	3½hrs	Easy	No	Yes	119
17	Shalfleet to Newport	19.9km (12.4 miles)	6½hrs	Fairly easy	Yes	Yes	124
18	Gatcombe to Newport	9km (5.6 miles)	2½hrs	Moderate	No	Yes	130
19	Tennyson Trail	14.9km (9.3 miles)	5hrs	Moderate	No	No	135

EAST WIGHT							
Walk no.	Walk title	Distance	Time	Grade	Refreshments en route?	Early finish option?	Page
20	Shanklin circular via Nettlecombe	24.3km (15.2 miles)	9hrs	Moderate–strenuous	Very limited	Yes	140
21	Shanklin circular via Bonchurch	9.4km (5.9 miles)	3½hrs	Moderate	Yes	Yes	149
22	Shanklin circular via America Wood	8.2km (5.1 miles)	3hrs	Moderate–strenuous	No	Yes	154
23	Shanklin to Godshill	7.4km (4.6 miles)	2½hrs	Fairly easy	No	Yes	158
24	Niton circular via The Undercliff	6.5km (4.1 miles)	2hrs	Moderate	Yes	Yes	161
25	Niton circular via St Catherine's Down	8km (5 miles)	2½hrs	Moderate	No	Yes	164
26	Ashey station circular	12.6km (7.9 miles)	4½hrs	Moderate–strenuous	At alternative start/finish only	Limited	167
27	Ryde to Ventnor	26.3km (16.4 miles)	9hrs	Easy–strenuous	Yes	Yes	171
28	Seaview circular	18.1km (11.3 miles)	6hrs	Moderate	Yes	Yes	179
29	Wootton Bridge circular	15.9km (10 miles)	5½hrs	Fairly easy	Yes	Limited	185
30	Wootton Bridge to Newport	9.4km (5.9 miles)	3hrs	Easy	Yes	Yes	189
31	Bembridge Trail	19.8km (12.4 miles)	6½hrs	Fairly easy–moderate	Yes	Yes	194
32	Worsley Trail	20km (12.5 miles)	7hrs	Moderate	Yes	Yes	201
33	Shorwell to Brading	20.4km (12.8 miles)	7½hrs	Moderate–strenuous	Yes	Yes	208
34	Godshill to Ventnor	7.4km (4.6 miles)	3hrs	Moderate	No	Yes	215

*Tearoom inside attraction (admission fee)

APPENDIX B
Useful contacts

Tourist Information

The official tourist website at www.islandbreaks.co.uk has a wealth of up-to-date information including current events, accommodation and where to eat. The council also operates a tourism telephone service – 01983 813813.

Visitor information is provided year-round at the bus stations in Ryde, Newport and Yarmouth, as well as the 'Seasons' store in Ventnor High Street. Mobile tourist information vans also operate in summer in Sandown, Shanklin and Cowes.

For more detailed information, look at the weekly Isle of Wight County Press (www.iwcp.co.uk), and do check out Matt & Cat's frank and witty personal reviews of the island's eateries at www.mattandcat.co.uk/reviews.

Transport

Ferries

Wightlink www.wightlink.co.uk
Tel: 0871 376 1000; email via website

Red Funnel www.redfunnel.co.uk
Tel: 0844 844 9988;
email: post@redfunnel.co.uk

Hovercraft

Hovertravel www.hovertravel.co.uk
Tel: 08434 87 88 87;
email: info@hovertravel.com

Buses

Southern Vectis www.islandbuses.info
Tel: 0871 200 2233;
email: talk2us@islandbuses.info
(See 'Getting around' in the introduction for an indication of current daily frequency.)

Train

Island Line www.southwesttrains.co.uk
Tel: 0845 6000 650 (South West Trains);
email via website

Parking

Car park locations and charges
(search www.iwight.com)

Tide times

Search the Isle of Wight County Press website (www.iwcp.co.uk)

Libraries (including internet access)

Search www.iwight.com

Island societies

Isle of Wight Natural History and Archaeological Society
www.iwnhas.org

Hampshire & Isle of Wight Wildlife Trust
www.hwt.org.uk

Biodiversity www.wildonwight.co.uk

LISTING OF CICERONE GUIDES

GR20: Corsica
Mont Blanc Walks
Mountain Adventures in
  the Maurienne
The Cathar Way
The GR5 Trail
The Robert Louis
  Stevenson Trail
Tour of the Oisans: The GR54
Tour of the Queyras
Tour of the Vanoise
Trekking in the Vosges and Jura
Vanoise Ski Touring
Walking in the Auvergne
Walking in the Cathar Region
Walking in the Cevennes
Walking in the Dordogne
Walking in the Haute Savoie
  North & South
Walking in the Languedoc
Walking in the Tarentaise and
  Beaufortain Alps
Walking on Corsica

GERMANY
Germany's Romantic Road
Walking in the Bavarian Alps
Walking in the Harz Mountains
Walking the River Rhine Trail

HIMALAYA
Annapurna
Bhutan
Everest: A Trekker's Guide
Garhwal and Kumaon: A
  Trekker's and Visitor's Guide
Kangchenjunga:
  A Trekker's Guide
Langtang with Gosainkund and
  Helambu: A Trekker's Guide
Manaslu: A Trekker's Guide
The Mount Kailash Trek
Trekking in Ladakh

ICELAND & GREENLAND
Trekking in Greenland
Walking and Trekking in Iceland

IRELAND
Irish Coastal Walks
The Irish Coast to Coast Walk
The Mountains of Ireland

ITALY
Gran Paradiso

Sibillini National Park
Stelvio National Park
Shorter Walks in the Dolomites
Through the Italian Alps
Trekking in the Apennines
Trekking in the Dolomites
Via Ferratas of the Italian
  Dolomites: Vols 1 & 2
Walking in Abruzzo
Walking in Sardinia
Walking in Sicily
Walking in the Central
  Italian Alps
Walking in the Dolomites
Walking in Tuscany
Walking on the Amalfi Coast
Walking the Italian Lakes

MEDITERRANEAN
Jordan – Walks, Treks, Caves,
  Climbs and Canyons
The Ala Dag
The High Mountains of Crete
The Mountains of Greece
Treks and Climbs in Wadi Rum,
  Jordan
Walking in Malta
Western Crete

NORTH AMERICA
British Columbia
The Grand Canyon
The John Muir Trail
The Pacific Crest Trail

SOUTH AMERICA
Aconcagua and the
  Southern Andes
Torres del Paine

SCANDINAVIA
Walking in Norway

SLOVENIA, CROATIA
AND MONTENEGRO
The Julian Alps of Slovenia
The Mountains of Montenegro
Trekking in Slovenia
Walking in Croatia
Walking in Slovenia:
  The Karavanke

SPAIN AND PORTUGAL
Costa Blanca: West
Mountain Walking in
  Southern Catalunya

The Mountains of Central Spain
The Northern Caminos
Trekking through Mallorca
Walking in Madeira
Walking in Mallorca
Walking in the Algarve
Walking in the
  Cordillera Cantabrica
Walking in the Sierra Nevada
Walking on La Gomera
  and El Hierro
Walking on La Palma
Walking on Tenerife
Walks and Climbs in
  the Picos de Europa

SWITZERLAND
Alpine Pass Route
Canyoning in the Alps
Central Switzerland
The Bernese Alps
The Swiss Alps
Tour of the Jungfrau Region
Walking in the Valais
Walking in Ticino
Walks in the Engadine

TECHNIQUES
Geocaching in the UK
Indoor Climbing
Lightweight Camping
Map and Compass
Mountain Weather
Moveable Feasts
Outdoor Photography
Polar Exploration
Rock Climbing
Sport Climbing
The Book of the Bivvy
The Hillwalker's Guide
  to Mountaineering
The Hillwalker's Manual

MINI GUIDES
Avalanche!
Navigating with a GPS
Navigation
Pocket First Aid and
  Wilderness Medicine
Snow

For full information on all our
guides, and to order books
and eBooks, visit our website:
www.cicerone.co.uk.

Walking – Trekking – Mountaineering – Climbing – Cycling

Over 40 years, Cicerone have built up an outstanding collection of 300 guides, inspiring all sorts of amazing adventures.

Every guide comes from extensive exploration and research by our expert authors, all with a passion for their subjects. They are frequently praised, endorsed and used by clubs, instructors and outdoor organisations.

All our titles can now be bought as **e-books** and many as iPad and Kindle files and we will continue to make all our guides available for these and many other devices.

Our website shows any **new information** we've received since a book was published. Please do let us know if you find anything has changed, so that we can pass on the latest details. On our **website** you'll also find some great ideas and lots of information, including sample chapters, contents lists, reviews, articles and a photo gallery.

It's easy to keep in touch with what's going on at Cicerone, by getting our monthly **free e-newsletter**, which is full of offers, competitions, up-to-date information and topical articles. You can subscribe on our home page and also follow us on **Facebook** and **Twitter**, as well as our **blog**.

Cicerone – the very best guides for exploring the world.

CICERONE

2 Police Square Milnthorpe Cumbria LA7 7PY
Tel: 015395 62069 info@cicerone.co.uk
www.cicerone.co.uk